Professional Learning Communities

Professional Learning Communities

The Ultimate Blueprint for Academic Success

Barbara D. Culp

ROWMAN & LITTLEFIELD
Lanham • Boulder • New York • London

Published by Rowman & Littlefield
An imprint of The Rowman & Littlefield Publishing Group, Inc.
4501 Forbes Boulevard, Suite 200, Lanham, Maryland 20706
www.rowman.com

6 Tinworth Street, London SE11 5AL, United Kingdom

Copyright © 2019 by Barbara D. Culp

All rights reserved. No part of this book may be reproduced in any form or by any electronic or mechanical means, including information storage and retrieval systems, without written permission from the publisher, except by a reviewer who may quote passages in a review.

British Library Cataloguing in Publication Information Available

Library of Congress Cataloging-in-Publication Data Available

ISBN: 978-1-4758-4533-4 (cloth : alk. paper)
ISBN: 978-1-4758-4534-1 (pbk. : alk. paper)
ISBN: 978-1-4758-4535-8 (electronic)

This book is dedicated to the progressive school districts and schools across the globe that are currently embracing professional learning communities and those seeking to pursue the PLC line of thinking. It is a serious, yet rewarding undertaking, and the benefits for districts, schools, and students are enormous and measurable. Kudos to those leading the charge and deeply passionate about what the future holds for PLCs. Your persistence and perseverance will *get you there. Inside this blueprint, I guide you step-by-step to PLC academic success!*

Alone we can do so little; together we can do so much.

—Helen Keller

Contents

Foreword *Heather E. Blackmon*	xiii
Preface	xv
Acknowledgments	xix
Introduction	xxi

1 LAY THE FOUNDATION — 1
   Building Blocks
      Reflective Practices — 2
      Focus on Learning
      Dialog — 3
      Shared Responsibility
      Shared Values and Norms — 4
      Common Practice
      Feedback — 5
   Creating a PLC
      Collaboration and Trust
      Inclusiveness and Shared Responsibility — 7
      Focus on Solutions
      Step-by-Step — 8
         Set a Schedule
         Select a Facilitator
         Define the Environment — 9

Build Your Home	
Revitalize an Existing PLC	10
People Come First	
Inform New Members	
Reach Out	11
Celebrate	
Building Blocks for a Professional Learning Community	12
An Accord to Open Every PLC Meeting	13
Questionnaire for Every PLC Member	
Questionnaire for the Start of New Initiatives	14
Stretches to Enhance Group Response	
Stretch 1: Build It Up	15
Stretch 2: Break It Down	
Stretch 3: Bring It Together	
Stretch 4: Identify Benefits	
Stretch 5: Identify Challenges	
Stretch 6: Eliminate Obstacles	
Notes	16

2 GATHER THE GOALS — 17

The Educational Forest	
Find the Microclimates	18
Specify the Species	20
How Does Your Forest Grow?	
Embrace Exotics	21
Cultivate Individual Plots	22
Forest Management	23
Slings and Arrows (Goal Sheets)	24
Goal Prompts	26
Broad Goals	
Specific Goals	
Unique and Short-Term Goals	27
Professional Learning Goals for Members	28
Notes	

3 GOING LIVE — 31

Begin at the Beginning	
Planning for Success	32
Develop the Program	33
Teacher Portfolios	34
Call on the Community	35
Personalize Implementation	
Collegial Implementation	36

	Return to the Beginning	37
	Link the Connection Points	38
	Team Goals	39
	Essential Outcomes	
	Milestone Achievements	40
	Comparison Points	
	Resource List	41
	Lesson Plan Template	42
	Student Feedback	43
	Portfolio Tips	
	Personalize the Plan	44
	Notes	45
4	ASSESS AND ADAPT	47
	How Many and How Often	
	Assessing the Data	48
	A Supportive Approach	49
	Assessment Foundation	50
	Types of Assessments	51
	Building the Formative Assessment	52
	Avoid Assessment Bias	
	Analyze and Assess Prompts for Data Collection	53
	Common Formative Assessments	54
	Summative Assessment Tips	55
	Assess the Assessment	
	PLC Assessment for Schools	56
	PLC Assessment for Members	57
	Key Markers for Success	58
	Notes	59
5	DIGITAL EXPANSION	61
	The Value of an Online Presence	
	Initial Online Presence	62
	Expanding Your Online Presence	63
	Documents and Files	64
	Collective Efforts	65
	Adapt Digital Tools	66
	Digital Tools for the Classroom	67
	Instant Updates and Motivation	
	Tips for Sharing	68
	Tips for Collaboration	
	Tips for Collective Digital Efforts	
	Assessing Digital Tools	69

	Common Classroom Digital Tools	70
	Top Digital Tools for PLCs	71
	Notes	
6	SAIL ON COURSE	73
	Information Indigestion	
	Wilting Enthusiasm	74
	Dysfunctional Roles	75
	Why PLCs Fail	76
	Avoid a Major Crisis	77
	Climate Control	78
	Best Research Practices	79
	Recharge the PLC	
	Team Trust Survey	80
	Exercises for Building Trust	
	Course Adjustments	81
	District-Wide Impact	82
	Notes	83

Appendix: Stepping onto the PLC Highway	86
Refresher 1: Lay the Foundation	
Refresher 2: Gather the Goals	
Refresher 3: Going Live	87
Refresher 4: Assess and Adapt	
Refresher 5: Digital Expansion	88
Refresher 6: Sail on Course	89
About the Author	91

Foreword

In the fall of 1992, I became a high school social studies teacher. I was teaching civics and economics to ninth-grade students in a highly competitive school with an excellent reputation for preparing students for the future. I learned very quickly that my value as a teacher from that point on would be judged primarily on my students' scores on standardized, end-of-course tests. I watched as teachers closed their doors at the start of class, and kept activities and resources locked away in filing cabinets to which they held the only key. It was as if they were sworn to protect plans, activities, and resources so that they could show higher student performance than other teachers at the end of the year. To say that teaching took place in isolation would be an understatement.

Fortunately, within about five years, the work of educational reformists such as Michael Fullan, Robert and Rebecca Du Four, and Robert Eaker began to take hold across the country, and we learned quickly that when teachers and systems work together, student achievement increased. It made sense that two, three, five, or fifteen heads were better than one when it came to the teaching and learning process.

As the idea of professional learning communities (PLCs) became better defined and the goals of these entities became more concrete, we were provided some professional development for a few days and then were charged as teachers to implement PLCs in our school. I enjoyed my colleagues, and we set up times to meet on a regular basis. These very first PLC meetings were wonderful times for us to share frustrations about students, the administration, the lack of copiers in the building, and the size of the faculty restrooms. We may have understood the theory, but at that point, the norms and routines that we needed to follow in order to gain higher student achievement were still very convoluted.

As I entered administration in 2007, the literature and training on the work of PLCs had grown dramatically, and I was able to look at the PLC work in my new school from a different perspective. These meetings seemed much more productive, as teachers were planning together, sharing resources, and helping new teachers with curriculum mapping and ideas for teaching students. Still, there was no real way to measure student growth and achievement until the end of the semester, when it was too late to alter the teaching and learning process for these students.

When I became a principal of a high school in 2014, I was armed with data, common formative assessments, the concepts of reteaching and reassessing, and a basic template that teachers could use in their meetings to keep the discussion centered on students and the concept of mastery of objectives. I found quickly that some professional learning communities were much more functional than others. I saw that teachers who brought student work, as well as student scores to the table began to have greater success. When we set up a lunch tutorial system, my best PLC teams used that time to group students into areas for prescriptive remediation and review based upon areas where students had yet to achieve mastery. It was in these teams that I saw student achievement soar at the end of that semester and continue to grow over my next three years.

What we didn't have were specific "play-by-play" steps and activities that could be applied to PLC teams across the school curriculum. The assessments that were evaluated by biology teachers did not exactly fit the mold that the cultural arts and physical educational teams needed to use. I am delighted to say that this work by Barbara D. Culp is what school leaders and teachers have longed for, with templates and guides that ensure that teachers can use the cycle of data analysis at each PLC meeting, and then take the action steps necessary for documentation of student learning. Our teachers are very much like our students. They often need an "exemplar" of a final product in order to set a track for their team. This book does an exemplary job of taking theory and converting it to practical steps that can guide any professional learning community. We know that it works. This book is a fantastic "how to" resource for creating effective Professional Learning Communities.

Heather E. Blackmon
Former Principal
Director, JNCG
Communities in Schools

Preface

Educators are a diverse lot. Peer inside any school and you'll find fresh graduates of teaching programs who are eager to engage. You'll also watch seasoned professionals convey knowledge using decades of experience as instructors. Beside them are the administrators who ensure that the operations flow smoothly.

These people come from every walk of life. They stand beside the students who are our future. Every one of those educational professionals is an explorer. Their love of new ideas, their desire for groundbreaking techniques, and their heartfelt optimism run deep. They strive for the best for the young minds in their care as well as the surrounding neighborhoods.

For more than forty years, I have been a part of our diverse educational community. As a teacher, principal, tutor, and parent, my efforts have focused on the evolution of education. Small steps and big leaps have been a part of my path, as they are a part of yours.

No matter what type of project I turned to or where my career took me, professional learning communities proved to be a pipeline to success. These groups lift academic achievement reliably, consistently, and with the excellence we should demand for every student.

Improvement is every educator's first and continuous goal. By setting up a learning community, you and your peers will be taking the single step that can generate true greatness in your schools.

PLCs are, as their name implies, communities. Because learning groups invite individuals from every part of the school system, they are themselves diverse. With this broad base of wisdom to draw on, learning communities become more than the teachers who develop the programs, and more than the administrators who manage resources.

PLCs draw together the best that a district has to offer. Inside the meetings, they create spaces where individuals can openly share, discuss, plan, and network. Learning communities are nothing less than Olympic-level teams focused on academic achievement.

As you create and maintain your own professional learning group, be prepared for big things to happen. The sense of isolation that plagues so many teachers will be replaced with comradery and deep connections. Areas of the school's culture that are problematic will be corrected.

Academic opportunities will be available to every learner. Parents will feel confident and grateful that such a passionate group is championing the most important aspect of their children's lives. The dedication and professionalism that draw so many to become educators will be nourished with a richness beyond measure.

Because PLCs are open to parents, administrators, and even students, they can change elements that cause seemingly intractable issues. The impact of family issues, economic downturns, and other events that occur off campus can be alleviated. When everyone who is affected becomes involved in an educational learning community, the results benefit everyone in the neighborhoods served by those schools.

When I consider how PLCs work, I can't help thinking back to the days of the one-room schoolhouse. Although the original school structure was determined by elements we don't deal with today, the old-fashioned setup provided a handful of exceptional benefits.

With so few students in the classroom, teachers were able to provide individual attention. Educators often knew the students' families as well as the children and could reach out to tackle issues that impacted academic performance. The ties were closely knit, and everyone tried to help everyone else.

A learning community provides those same intimate benefits to our schools. The members develop projects and programs based on conditions in their district, their student populations, and their classrooms. The specific needs of the different families they serve are known, which leads to the development of tools tailored to their region.

As the professional learning community grows, its members learn more about each other as well as the populations they serve. They are able to respond more quickly when events begin to affect academic progress. Since they understand each other so well, they are able to help in ways that government mandates can never hope to achieve.

Many people think of PLCs as places where teachers can supercharge their skills. This is true. And yet, a learning community offers so much more. With a focus on academic achievement and access for every student, it serves the young minds that will build our future.

With a PLC's profound benefits come profound changes. The learning community turns the attention of parents and even business leaders to the schools in their neighborhoods. As support for the group grows, support for educational initiatives also grows. Individuals who might not otherwise get involved are motivated to pitch in.

By sharing leadership roles, working collaboratively, and creating supportive conditions, learning communities work toward a shared vision. Their helping hands link them together to create a strong and vibrant group. They ensure that every student is given the same access to educational opportunities. They ensure that their schools will thrive along with the larger community.

Nothing that I know of will take you farther than a professional learning community. Everything that has ever proven effective for students has become a keystone for effective PLCs. The largest paradigm shift I have seen in my forty-plus years as an educator is happening right now because of these groups.

I'm so glad you've decided to join the revolution. Through this book, I am reaching out to help you with every step of the process. You will strike off on your own very often because exploration and experimentation are embedded in PLCs. You'll also find that each new pathway is paved with the same building blocks laid out in these pages.

Every morning, parents send their kids off to school. When the doors open, students pour in and take their seats. The staff has prepared the campus and tends to its operations. And then the teacher steps in front of the classroom and leads the way into a bright future.

What an exciting journey you are already on. Make the most of the work you've already done, and build a community of like-minded professionals who will explore new roads. At every turn, you will know exactly where to go because you have the support and experience of your PLC as your foundation.

Acknowledgments

I offer a special thank-you to the many effective teachers whose professional work, posture, and attitude over the years stayed with me so that I could incorporate the memory of their dedication into the pages of this book. You gave me so much to write about. I remember the lengths you went to in order to ensure that the children's lives you touched got the *best* education you could possibly give them. Many of you made the ultimate sacrifice, choosing teaching over family. You begged, borrowed, purchased, and teamed with like-minded teachers to give students your best!

Also, I want to sincerely thank my dear friend Laine Cunningham, who once again guided another one of my books to a finished product, one that I am proud to present to the world. I could not do what I do without you. You are my sunshine!

I also wish to express my heartfelt thanks and appreciation to Dr. Earle D. Clowney, retired (university editor), for being my "editor in residence." He makes sure my manuscripts are print ready when sent to the publisher.

Introduction

A professional learning community (PLC) is any organization that utilizes reflective practices to enhance the professional abilities of its members. The highest mission of educational learning communities is academic achievement. Every step they take is geared toward maximizing the advancement of educational goals.

Often these groups are formed by dedicated individuals who want to move their schools and communities forward. They volunteer to join an existing PLC, or they come together to form their own group. During my forty-plus years in education, I saw a number of these groups function inside the schools. Not until I approached retirement were they given an official name that reflected their mission and their devotion: professional learning communities.

PLCs can focus on any number of areas. Their mission statements can be broad, or they can come together to work in specific areas where their schools need support. Generally, however, PLCs are committed to enhancing curriculum while helping the staff become better at their jobs.

Teachers are naturally drawn to PLCs. The groups have room for many types of members, however. Frequently learning communities include administrators. Ones that reach out frequently to students might see a handful of teenagers join their ranks. The group might also expand into the community through outreach to parents, nonprofits, and local businesses.

This broad inclusiveness ensures that a diverse variety of voices are heard. The school community boasts a range of life experiences, cultures, and backgrounds. A PLC that includes individuals from many professions and different walks of life will be better able to serve its target populations.

The wide reach also points to the PLC's heart, which beats through the relationships it forms. Every individual within the group, no matter their background, shares certain values relating to education. They join together to implement those ideals in classrooms and schools. They focus on learning rather than teaching, which enhances their ability to reach students from every background.

The members of a PLC also hold themselves accountable for the results that arise from their efforts. Reflecting on the impact of their efforts is a critical part of the process. Reflection reveals better ways to reach goals. By applying this process to every step, PLCs offer enormous benefits to their schools and their students.

The teachers and other group members benefit, too. These gains arise in no small part from the PLC's culture. The thoughtfully considered action taken to solve problems builds and supports this culture. Each effort made by the group therefore serves to clarify the values held by the group.

This culture, over time, transforms the group and each of its members. It also transforms the culture of the school, the administrative procedures, and the atmosphere of the larger community. The positive, can-do attitude along with the total dedication to excellence flows outward. Every element touched by the PLC is lifted on the same tide.

I spent decades in public education as a teacher and principal. After training as a superintendent, my role turned toward a tutoring company I founded. Because I wanted to reach educators, I wrote a series of books targeting different professionals in the field. And because students and parents are such an intrinsic part of the academic process, I also wrote titles targeting those audiences.

Every one of those books demonstrates the single value I hold most dear: a dedication to a quality education for our nation's youth. Today's students are tomorrow's parents, counselors, business managers, and political leaders. The foundation of our country rests squarely, not on what teachers attempt to impart, but on what those students actually learn.

In this book, I am going to ask several things of you. First and foremost, I will ask you to be dedicated, fully and deeply, to real learning in the classroom. Next, I ask that you be willing to recognize and examine the issues at your school. Be open to finding new ways to address those challenges.

In a real sense, every professional learning group is a coalition of explorers. Experimentation and a sense of the opportunities that await you are key. Always question the status quo, even if things appear to be running smoothly. Always hear the voices of others whose backgrounds and experiences are different from your own.

Improvement should be your first and continuous goal. Self-assessment, an impartial assessment of your peers, and a realistic approach are your indispensable tools. Honesty about how well each milestone is reached and the overall success of your effort is critical.

Finally, please be willing to be part of a team. PLCs are communities. Every community member must make compromises to ensure that the community's needs are met. I promise you that the more you give of yourself, the more your PLC will give to you.

If you can bring an attitude of openness and careful evaluation to the table, then you are ready for the blueprint for PLC success. This book lays out the process of creating, maintaining, and sustaining a learning community. Even if you are part of an established group, you will find plenty of wisdom in the chapters that cover how to set up a PLC.

We will start by laying the foundation. The basis of every successful PLC is supported by its structure. Your group should have an official facilitator to run the meetings as well as a clear idea of how each member will contribute. Trust, one of the most important elements for long-term success, is built through professionalism and confidentiality.

You will discover that the core of every PLC is inclusion. Too often, isolation can prevent educators from providing the best for their students and their schools. The learning group offers a powerful way to open up your school to the best that your community has to offer. Guidelines for creating your first PLC or for restructuring an existing PLC will ensure that inclusion is built into every element of your group.

Then we will gather the goals. The goals of a PLC might seem self-evident. In a way, that is true; staff excellence and student achievement are clearly primary goals. However, these large goals can be so broad that achievement becomes fuzzy. Measuring your achievements becomes difficult.

To prevent this fuzziness, each goal should be divided into a series of smaller goals that will be met along the way. This approach makes success more likely. It also enhances the ability of the PLC to function at full capacity. Chapter 2 provides examples of common PLC goals and breaks them down into standard smaller goals.

In order to be effective, the information shared at PLC meetings needs to be implemented in the classroom. Chapter 3, "Going Live," will lay out how your group can select the ideas that will work best, given the circumstances. A variety of common situations will be described, and materials are provided to help you implement your group's goals.

Then we move into the core component of truly great PLCs. In chapter 4, "Assess and Adapt," we consider what works and what doesn't. By looking at common situations, we can determine why some efforts fail and others succeed. The techniques in this chapter can be adapted to different learning environments for optimal positive impact.

One step that helps PLCs expand their success rate is including other schools. Digital tools are one of the easiest ways to implement effective outreach. You begin within your district and can later expand to other districts in your state. The influx of new ideas and different perspectives supercharges a group's creativity, morale, and dedication.

Social media and blog posts, a basic form of outreach, provide feeds and information that anyone can dip into as often as they like. Midlevel sharing options include exchanging materials with other PLCs. The top level can implement statewide sharing and communication as well as connect with districts nationwide.

Finally, this book will teach you how to stay focused on the PLC's original goals over time; this can be particularly challenging in an educational environment.

Chapter 6, "Sail On Course," offers ideas, techniques, and solutions for early, mid-range, and long-term challenges and timelines.

By that point, you will understand how the different elements of a PLC interlink, and how they can be harnessed to face critical events. My goal is to launch you into your own learning community equipped with the ideas, techniques, and confidence you need to succeed.

Using these tools, you will discover what you need to teach, what you need to reteach, and who needs to be taught. You will learn how to develop the tools that can uncover why students struggle. And you will be able to build solutions that place academic excellence within reach of every learner.

The guidance in this book helps you meet these goals as a group based on trust and respect. Your openness to improvements will show you the way forward. The leadership offered to you inside the PLC as well as your group's ability to lead within the district will grow.

This guidance is not given from inside a theoretical bubble. The real experiences of PLCs from across the nation, as well as my own decades of experience, have been mined to provide actionable steps and plenty of resources. Each chapter ends with a collection of charts, worksheets, checklists, and tips that can be used immediately.

Since you are reading this book, I know you already have a deep sense of commitment to the future of your school. You are genuinely interested in improving your ability to reach students where they are. You are dedicated to guiding them toward the rich intellectual achievements they so clearly deserve.

Along the way, you will discover that your professional learning community can lift you and your school in ways you could not accomplish on your own. That is the beating heart of every PLC: the understanding that, together, we can achieve so much more than we can alone.

1

Lay the Foundation

To a large degree, the success of every PLC springs from its structure. The important elements include a facilitator, an alternate facilitator who can occasionally step into the lead, and a clear definition of how each member will contribute. These relationships build trust within the group through professionalism and an understanding that conversations are confidential.

A successful PLC is built with the fullest breadth of inclusion. The desire to reach deeply into the community ensures that all voices are heard. The isolation that can prevent educators from providing the best for their students and their schools is eliminated in the same gesture.

In this chapter, you'll find useful guidelines for creating a PLC that can serve your school's specific needs. Guidance for restructuring an existing PLC can help readers who are just now stepping into an existing group. The advice also provides useful guidance on elements that can be added to an existing learning community's procedures.

Every group grows and changes as it moves forward. For learning communities, that reality is ever present. It can be challenging; ultimately, the group that adapts to the changing needs of the student population is the one that succeeds. This chapter will empower your group to meet the demands.

BUILDING BLOCKS

Before a professional learning community can come together, its members must understand the individual components that drove its creation. These components include the values by which every action should be measured. They also encompass the specific activities through which PLCs implement powerful, positive change.

Each of the primary elements will be described in this section. While the descriptions provide a complete overview and can be utilized as they stand, they can also be easily modified to fit the specific needs of your learning community. Your group can begin with these core characteristics and modify them as you move forward or swap out existing elements with ones described here.

Reflective Practices

Reflective practices are the living, beating heart of every professional learning community. Each activity is examined to determine how well that activity met stated goals. By measuring the process as well as the outcome against stated goals, PLCs supercharge their results.

Reflecting on actions ensures that experience leads to true learning. Performing an action, even if the results are positive, does not necessarily lead to growth. When the group takes the time to examine an activity, gather feedback, and consider how to adjust future actions based on this new understanding, the goals of the group can be more easily realized.

Reflection provides insights that might otherwise slip away unnoticed. Capturing information about a process provides a deeper understanding of how individuals and the group work. Importantly, these insights can be preserved and transmitted to other members or other PLCs. Everyone learns through lived experiences.

In the PLC, just as inside the classroom, reflective steps function as data-gathering and analysis tools. Lessons learned can refocus attention on values, change behaviors, and lead to a deeper commitment. Best of all, each member gains insight into their own approach.

At the end of the process, professionals discover that their commitment has been refreshed and recharged. They can undertake the next task knowing that they have better tools, more expansive abilities, and greater confidence in their ability to create change. They achieve and exceed previous levels of excellence.

Focus on Learning

Professional learning communities place an emphasis on *learning rather than teaching*. Through this lens, hasty conclusions that do not reveal the realities of the educational atmosphere are eliminated. A systematic approach considers how students are learning and how teachers are implementing instruction.

PLCs work so well in part because they emphasize, continually and efficiently, how things can get better. In too many educational situations, a reform or change is initially met with enthusiasm. As efforts get under way, however, classrooms find themselves hampered by unclear objectives or uneven application. What started out heralded by trumpets crumbles to dust.

By maintaining a focus on professional learning, your group eliminates the pitfalls associated with flagging support. Each initiative achieves more than the one before. Sustained energy and effort uncover better ways to reach goals A true cycle of change—one that results in positive effects and beneficial achievements—is built. The educational community reaps the rewards.

Dialog

PLCs encourage and support *dialog among educators.* Rather than coming to the table with preconceived notions, individuals who share their thoughts and ideas discover new perspectives. They receive valuable information that, through no fault of their own, might otherwise never touch their sphere.

Importantly, dialog allows individuals to adjust their positions in ways that empower them to meet new challenges. Education as a whole is constantly challenged with changing elements and shifting resources. The creativity and interconnectivity generated by dialog offers a significant channel through which to address issues.

This interchange is one of the most dynamic elements of any professional learning community. A diversity of experience breathes fresh air into stale structures. Inclusivity is truly supported and maintained, which in turn opens up new resources and uncovers new pathways. From the daily class to the broader community, dialog among educators is a powerful force for change.

Shared Responsibility

If reflective practices are the heart of a professional learning community, then *shared responsibility* is the blood that oxygenates its limbs. Even today, most schools place a single teacher alone in a room with a group of students. Educators are only able to join together during short breaks during the day or at intermittently scheduled programs throughout the year.

This results in isolation so deep that sharing thoughts, ideas, successes, and perspectives becomes difficult. Garnering feedback from others is also challenging. Explaining an issue can only be done using terms associated with the individual teacher's experience. This limits the ability of others to pinpoint the true obstacle.

Additionally, implementing collaborative efforts becomes extraordinarily problematic. Educators have trouble finding others with whom to collaborate, let alone professionals who can offer the wisdom they require. Without collaborative opportunities, individuals have access to far fewer professional learning experiences.

The solution is the shared responsibility found in a professional learning community. By joining together, educators can challenge the status quo. Together, they can implement adjustments to better serve the staff and the students. By mobilizing around shared values, they draw others into a shared mission and successfully meet goals.

A culture of shared responsibility generates real and lasting changes. The atmosphere becomes one of continuous learning, shared decision making, and leadership undertaken by all members. The learning group's members gain professionally. The students gain academically.

Shared Values and Norms

A PLC should encourage *shared values and norms* among its members. Here we need to look at both elements separately to understand how they work together. While many individuals speak about values and norms as if they are the same, they are different in important ways.

Values are abstract concepts about what is important. The values held by the group point to specific elements or things they feel are worthy of their resources. When a group holds the same values, every member of the group remains focused on the same goals. They agree more often on where to spend their valuable time and effort. Their activities become self-supported and are therefore more effective.

It's important, then, for a PLC to define its values early in its creation. Think of values as general guidelines that will direct both the group and individual members. While values are frequently codified in mission statements, they are displayed clearly in how the group moves forward with individual goals and tasks. Every step taken by the PLC should utilize the stated set of values.

Values should be clearly defined. Clear and specific values help those who are not part of the group understand the PLC's mission. When these values are broadcast by how the learning community operates, they attract likeminded individuals as new members. The PLC grows and expands simply by demonstrating its value system through its actions.

Norms, on the other hand, can be thought of as the group's culture. These guidelines tend to be more specific in how they are recorded as well as their impact on the group's activities. This is because norms define how the members should behave.

Norms lay out expectations about the attitude expected for a learning community's members. A dedication to positive, forward-thinking openness and honesty keeps the energy high. By strengthening this type of attitude within the group, every member radiates a powerful, influential impression when they are away from the group.

Discuss the rules, guidelines, and expectations of the PLC to create the norms expected for each member. This clear structure will help your group reach its goals in a cohesive fashion.

Common Practice

A professional learning community helps educators develop *common practices*. No matter whether your district provides detailed oversight or allows a decentralized approach, your group can create beneficial common practices within your schools.

A study by the Stanford Center for Opportunity Policy in Education (SCOPE)[1] discovered that providing common instructional standards enhanced the focus on instruction. In Milwaukee schools, noticeable gains were made with mathematics achievements. Modest gains were made in reading levels.

One additional benefit was that the district became much more supportive of teaching and learning. The development of common practices showed promising results in this small study. It can do the same for your learning community. When practices are developed over time, the results have the potential to grow.

Note that the SCOPE researchers felt that overcoming a culture of autonomy was difficult. In order for the learning community to truly bring people together, communication and the ongoing development of a shared vision was thought to be key. Your group can help your district and your schools by developing common practices.

Feedback

In researching how a PLC's feedback impacts educational staff, a study[2] considered ten individuals in various positions. Comments and concerns presented by the teachers at a Wisconsin high school spurred the administration to change key elements related to how students learned. The resources made available for teaching were also changed.

These adjustments shifted the culture of the school. The atmosphere became more conducive to teaching and learning. Teachers ended up with more support, and the academic results were favorable. The number of failing grades was reduced by 80 percent.

How can such a simple thing as providing comments have such a significant impact? The answer is simple. When comments come from the individuals who are in the trenches every day, the feedback is likely to be on target for the exact needs of the school's population. No one knows the students better than the educators who work with them day in and day out.

When the administration took action based on the feedback, they gave students and teachers exactly what they needed. They also shifted the discussion by reaching out to the ones who know best. They empowered the teachers to lobby for necessary changes. The culture became an inclusive one in which all voices were heard.

This is only one of the positive elements to be garnered through feedback. When the process is nonjudgmental and nonevaluative, members can listen and learn without fear that comments will end up in their employment files. Freedom engenders honesty, and change occurs more quickly.

CREATING A PLC

Collaboration and Trust

Professional learning communities thrive when all members collaborate to create the best possible outcomes. When setting up a group for the first time, then, leaders should ask for input about best practices, goals, and procedures. By collaborating to create the structure of the PLC, the group puts into practice one of its greatest strengths.

The atmosphere of working together and inclusivity sets the tone for everything that comes afterward. This builds the trust that is the lifeblood of the group. Individuals need to know that everything they offer, from words to actions, will meet with respect.

This element of a learning community cannot be overstated. Nothing should be held back for fear that confidentiality will be breached. Concerns should never be smothered because comments might make fellow educators, students, or parents view them as anything other than consummate professionals.

To foster this kind of openness, Anne Smith of the Mattituck-Cutchogue School District (New York) says that leaders "have to be clear that the goal is collaboration and not competition."[3] By building an environment in which individuals can share the obstacles they are trying to overcome, positive solutions can be developed.

To generate trust and build a collaborative culture in the group, all members should support the efforts of others. Individuals should take responsibility for solving problems. They should accept the consequences of their actions . . . as well as any failure to act.

Additionally, all members should agree to freely share ideas, perspectives, and experiences. This type of sharing is a true gift. It allows others to benefit from the best lessons learned. Members can steer around the pitfalls that others have encountered. A synergy that allows for real exchange develops quickly.

To this end, a variety of steps will enhance the function and efficacy of your PLC:

- Present information in user-friendly formats. Break financial or budgetary items into tables or charts. Use clear language, and support your ideas with examples of real-world efforts or theories that have been researched.
- Provide information through channels that are easy to disseminate, like a weekly email bulletin.
- Ensure that the information is available for later reference. For example, maintain a database on a shared electronic folder that can be accessed from any computer or cellphone.
- Even if a message requires a great deal of information to be exchanged, offer the key points in a bulleted list. This cements the important elements in memory. Later, members will be able to quickly recall the highlights.

While using these forms of communication, remember that the PLC will be best served through face-to-face encounters. Regular gatherings do not have to be highly formalized. The group might have a standard monthly meeting, for example, with informal weekly gatherings that occur in different places.

The formal monthly format provides a set structure for offering and considering ideas. Maintain minutes to ensure that agenda items are always seeing progress. Record keeping also ensures that new members can get up to speed quickly.

Meanwhile, the informal meetings allow for greater variety in the types of sharing that occur. As these smaller gatherings are likely to have different mixes of participants, core groups dedicated to specific activities can form on their own. They will be able to generate movement quickly because they will enjoy more time together.

Inclusiveness and Shared Responsibility

Inclusiveness and shared responsibility are separate elements. Yet they are so closely tied that they form a single loop through which all aspects of a strong PLC cycles. In this loop, members agree to share responsibility for their actions and the results; for members to agree on this, the group must be inclusive.

The atmosphere of inclusivity encourages every member to bear burdens alongside their fellows. This sharing of burdens enhances the feeling that every member shares responsibility. The results generated by this cycle are significant.

When the ribbons of inclusiveness and shared responsibility wrap around every part of a professional learning community, members know that their efforts are making a real difference. Even when results do not live up to expectations, adjustments that will lead to success arise from the group.

In this atmosphere, no effort is too large. No input is too small. Every task and activity undertaken by the group is performed well. When the group is accountable, milestones and goals are reached. Real change arrives inside the schools.

Interestingly, when these two elements twine throughout a learning community, the group ends up with greater freedom. Rather than be held back by worries about "what ifs," the group can lead the charge. No matter what happens along the way, they can call on the wisdom and teamwork of the group to adjust, adapt, and achieve.

Focus on Solutions

The entire reason a PLC comes together is to enact real and lasting change. Often this means that the group must tackle old, seemingly intractable issues with new minds. The power of the crowd, which is the core element of inclusivity, allows for unique opportunities to develop. The experiences of the diverse many generate creative ideas.

From these new thought processes, the causes and exacerbating factors relating to specific challenges are identified. Real solutions arise. Rather than treating a symptom or using stopgap measures, the problem (rather than its symptoms) can be tackled.

Every action, behavior, and resource associated with the issue can be laid out in detail. Each detail can be considered on its own as well as in terms of how it interacts with other details. The impact of changes can be discussed, and the likely outcomes can be thought through to the end. In this way, the best options become clear.

Step-by-Step

Once you have determined that a professional learning community will enhance your school, you need to implement the activities that will bring it to life. The following approach will guide your path so that every step results in the highest quality push right out of the starting gate.

Set a Schedule

Consider your school's approach to planning and cooperative efforts. In some places, you'll find that no slots have been provided on a daily or weekly basis for educators to gather. Other schools will be ahead of the game and will have allocated daily times during which staff can meet.

In schools that do not provide free time, consider how you can create space in the schedule. Would an early morning meeting be possible? Take over an empty conference room, and keep everyone on task so that teachers can be in the classroom on time. This can make meetings efficient because people have to get things done in order to end on time.

Meetings planned for after the regular school day offer different benefits and challenges. They can be more flexible in terms of meeting length, but might interfere with commitments for after-school activities.

If necessary, meetings can be scheduled to begin immediately after the day's extracurricular activities end. One benefit of this scheduling option is the time between class and the meeting. Individuals who don't have extracurricular activities can catch up on other tasks or finish their PLC deliverables before the meeting begins.

In every case, ensure that teachers who would not normally have the chance to meet other educators can join the PLC meetings. This is especially important in large schools and in organizations that don't dedicate time for collaboration.

The synergy created by the PLC will have immediate and long-term impacts. Once the benefits of creating that time are visible, administrators will be spurred to schedule free time into the following year's schedules.

Select a Facilitator

Many PLCs are begun by the same individual who acts as their facilitator. Quite naturally, the individual who first champions a learning community is often the one with the drive and the skills needed to bring people together. But the initiator does not have to become the facilitator.

A group can elect a leader and a second-in-command who will take the lead when the facilitator needs to be absent. Specific tasks undertaken by the PLC should have a different individual in charge of overseeing that task's goals. The responsibility is spread out among many. No one is overburdened, and everyone feeds the learning community's efforts.

Consider that the role of facilitator can be fulfilled by more than one individual and their backup. In this case, a group of individuals drawn from various backgrounds might lead the learning community at different times. Nothing provides a more powerful pathway to real change than a group led by diverse representatives who can speak with many voices.

Define the Environment

A professional learning community operates within a larger community that holds its own norms and values. That broader community also operates within a specific environment, and the overarching environment will have separate norms and values.

While building and maintaining your learning community, consider how your schools and the district operate. Some of the procedures that are already in place will support your PLC's efforts. Others might present barriers to your group's smooth operation.

Also, be aware of the culture of the community of parents. Individuals from different socioeconomic backgrounds will respond in different ways to the group's initiatives. Ensure that your approach is sensitive to their needs. Communicate through channels that are easy for them to access.

Recognize that the students are themselves a community. They will have built their own culture with its own values and norms. Know how your students view the school, its educators, and its staff. Find out, specifically and in detail, what students want from their schools.

Recognize that what students want might not be obvious. College-minded students from families suffering from economic difficulties might be at the top of the academic track yet still need assistance finding scholarships. Individuals who arrived from other schools might need access to study guides to keep their education on track.

To uncover the needs of students where they are right now, consider recruiting individuals from that population. Ask them for feedback on various issues. Have them head up polls and surveys. As your group implements changes that benefit the students, these representatives can become influencers who champion your efforts inside the student body.

Build Your Home

The core of an effective PLC is the educators who constantly strive to enhance their knowledge. They are already professionals in their field. Each one has something to offer. Encourage every member to define their strengths and weaknesses, and to share those with the group.

This simple step creates immediate channels between those who need help and those who can offer assistance. Individuals who are seeking to learn more in specific areas become empowered. They will be proactive in improving their skills because they know who has the wisdom they want. And they can ask for it in a supportive, nonjudgmental environment.

Recognize that, while professional development can be conducted through workshops and seminars, a PLC group learns at every meeting.[4] A school's development is intrinsically tied to the advancement of the teachers inside its classrooms. A district is uplifted when all the schools excel. The engine that drives this forward is the professional learning community.

It's *you*.

REVITALIZE AN EXISTING PLC

Once your group has been operating for a while, your learning community might want to hit the refresh button. Part of this might involve some level of restructuring. Even when you're just starting out, keep the tips in this section in mind as your group moves forward.

Considering the mission and approach of PLCs, facilitators can implement rejuvenation efforts at any time. As Charlie Coleman noted in his All Things PLC blog,[5] educators are unique in the professional world. Few career choices offer a regular time every year to step back from the crush of daily activities.

Summer or term breaks provide weeks or even months in which to recharge. These breaks are perfect times to reassess and plan adjustments within the PLC. Over time, mission statements can fade into the background, members might drop out or be transferred, and the influx of new members can unbalance operations.

At some point during the breaks, hold a special meeting to consider the previous year's activities. Focus on whether something about the operations or membership has fallen out of alignment. When issues arise, determine the best path forward by examining the areas listed here.

People Come First

Every school, district, and community is made up of people. The same is true of professional learning communities. Often, when a PLC is not meeting its goals or is encountering obstacles that deflate morale, a renewed focus on the group's members can help. Turning the spotlight on individuals can stabilize cohesion.

Inform New Members

People who join an existing group can feel a little disoriented or lost. Make sure that every member of a PLC understands the mission statement as well as the procedures. Over time, the meetings will demonstrate the structure codified in your group's operations. Provide this information to new members in writing so they can refer to the guidelines when questions arise.

A functioning PLC will know each member's areas of strength. Maintain a list of areas of expertise that each member can access. New members can immediately discover which individuals have the experience that will boost their learning efforts and help them achieve the group's goals.

The PLC's logs are a goldmine. They should list tasks that have been completed, results for each task, and the progress of ongoing assignments. These logs lay out the group's trajectory by tracing its history. With a quick review of ongoing tasks, new members can determine where they fit best. They can also comment on ongoing tasks and the results of completed tasks.

Always be sure to inform new members about the most recent successes. This will infuse the group with an energy that feeds current efforts. It can also spur ideas about additional ways to achieve the community's goals.

Reach Out

Ask for feedback and ideas from educators who are not currently members. Their perspectives might adjust the group's direction. With minor changes, the group's activities will remain aligned with actual needs.

Regular interactions with staff, from the bottom to the top, will deepen the wealth of viewpoints on which you can draw. You'll enhance inclusivity and hear from a wealth of diverse voices. Frequently this kind of outreach results in fresh ideas that can topple old obstacles that haven't yielded to the "tried and true" methods.

Target parents and students with separate outreach efforts. Parents often have ideas and access to opportunities outside the educational environment. They might not realize that the PLC is a perfect opportunity for their ideas and resources to be utilized. They might also have desires that remain unspoken because they don't know how to communicate with change makers.

Students are often a source of creative ideas. Because younger generations are less involved with the structures that command so much of life, they might recognize pathways that adults overlook. Listen to the students. You will surely find gems waiting to be unearthed.

Celebrate

Enhance the energy and joy your PLC creates by celebrating milestones. Announcements about goals that have been met, blog entries about positive results, posts about lessons learned, and the occasional press release can do wonders for morale.

When the group celebrates success, new members will want to join. Individuals who might not be able to dedicate an entire year to the group will pitch in on a temporary basis. An extra set of hands can be the difference between meeting a goal or falling short, so grab these easy opportunities to revitalize your group.

BUILDING BLOCKS FOR A PROFESSIONAL LEARNING COMMUNITY

Building Block	Benefits
Reflective Practice	• Considers how each activity met stated goals • Leads to true learning • Captures insights for a deeper understanding of individuals and the group dynamic • Allows members to learn from each other • Enhances data gathering • Generates deeper commitment
Focus on Learning	• Emphasizes learning over teaching • Uncovers the realities within the educational atmosphere • Provides a systematic process to consider how students are learning • Maintains a focus on improving the academic environment • Initiates and supports a cycle of true change
Dialog Among Educators	• Shares thoughts and ideas to develop new perspectives • Shifts old methods in ways that meet new challenges • Supports creativity and interconnectivity • Brings a diversity of experience to bear on issues • Discovers new resources and pathways
Shared Responsibility	• Allows feedback to be garnered more easily • Makes collaborative efforts easier to implement • Challenges the status quo more effectively • Implements adjustments more quickly • Generates real and lasting change • Shares decision making among all members
Shared Values	• Clearly indicate how efforts will be directed • Maintain a singular focus • Guide every step taken by the group • Help others understand the PLC's mission
Shared Norms	• Create the PLC's culture • Define how members will behave • Generate expectations about attitude
Common Practices	• Can be created in schools regardless of the district's approach • Enhance student learning through common instructional standards • Extract more district support based on academic results • Override the culture of autonomy that prevents sharing
Feedback	• Eliminates criticism in favor of beneficial advice • Exists outside the formal evaluation process • Eliminates negative impacts for individuals • Creates pathways for change to occur quickly • Broadens perspectives • Generates true change in how students learn • Strengthens learning outcomes for PLC members • Supports recommendations made to administrative staff by providing real-world data

AN ACCORD TO OPEN EVERY PLC MEETING

- All individuals agree to collaborate on the best possible outcomes.
- Trust building is an ongoing process.
- Inclusivity is a core component of the group's approach.
- A diversity of voices is encouraged.
- Confidentiality extends beyond the meeting room.
- Feedback and ideas will be welcomed in a spirit of acceptance.
- All members will support the efforts of all other members.
- Individuals take responsibility for the actions of the group.
- The group takes responsibility for the actions of each member.
- An atmosphere of sharing and caring will prevail.

QUESTIONNAIRE FOR EVERY PLC MEMBER

1. What skills and abilities can you bring to the group?
   _____
   _____

2. What skills and abilities can you identify in the facilitator?
   _____
   _____

3. What skills and abilities can you identify in other members?
   _____
   _____

4. What special characteristics of your school and district support the PLC's growth?
   _____
   _____

5. What elements of your school and district present obstacles to the PLC's mission?
   _____
   _____

6. How do you envision the PLC becoming involved in the school and/or district?
   _____
   _____

QUESTIONNAIRE FOR THE START OF NEW INITIATIVES

1. What types of resources will be required to implement this task successfully?
   _____
   _____

2. Are these resources already available? If not, how can they be sourced?
   _____
   _____

3. Which types of professional learning characteristics are required in order to move forward?
   _____
   _____

4. What types of existing programs can be utilized to enhance implementation of the task?
   _____
   _____

5. How will the needs of the school/district be met through this initiative?
   _____
   _____

STRETCHES TO ENHANCE GROUP RESPONSE

These exercises are intended to stretch the ways of thinking among individuals and the group as a whole. Utilize a brainstorming format for all of these.

Start by having group members jot all their ideas down on index cards, with one idea recorded on each card. The ideas are thrown into a box in the middle. Five minutes will be given for this step.

The facilitator then reads each card at random and writes its idea on a white board. When possible, ideas are recorded next to similar ideas.

New ideas can be added to the box as the facilitator works. Encourage the group to pull out all the stops. No idea should be considered too small or too complex.

Once all the cards have been read, the group will be able to see which ideas are held widely. They will also discover unique ideas that garner the support of the entire team.

Stretch 1: Build It Up

Start with the organizational structure of your school. Consider a specific task such as enhancing professional learning activities. Brainstorm about the ways the existing organizational structure can be utilized to achieve the task. If the existing structure needs to be rebuilt in part or in whole, detail point by point (one to a card) the specific changes that should be made.

Stretch 2: Break It Down

Consider the obstacles that challenge the successful completion of one goal. Brainstorm ways to circumvent or remove those obstacles. Utilize resources at hand as well as those that need to be captured.

Stretch 3: Bring It Together

Now that administrative pathways and the challenges of a task have been identified, determine how the PLC can proactively move toward the goal. Brainstorm the individual steps that need to happen at the beginning, middle, and end stages.

Stretch 4: Identify Benefits

Brainstorm all the possible benefits of the PLC's activity in relation to this specific task. Organize the results into a ranked list with no more than three primary goals. List a total of no more than five positive outcomes. These will be the primary focuses for the team's work.

Stretch 5: Identify Challenges

Brainstorm all the possible ways that successful achievement might be slowed or stopped. Rank the results in terms of likeliness.

Stretch 6: Eliminate Obstacles

Focus on the top three to five issues ranked as "most likely." Brainstorm ways to reduce their impact or eliminate them from the start.

The resulting list will empower the PLC to take preemptive steps before the task begins. The list will also alert members to anticipate certain challenges. These issues can then be proactively resolved if they start to arise.

NOTES

1. Montgomery, Ken, Darling-Hammond, Linda, and Campbell, Carol. *Developing Common Instructional Practice Across a Portfolio of Schools: The Evolution of School Reform in Milwaukee.* Stanford Center for Opportunity Policy in Education, 2011. Retrieved from https://edpolicy.stanford.edu/sites/default/files/publications/developing-common-instructional-practice-across-portfolio-schools-evolution-school-reform-milwaukee_0.pdf.

2. Roloff, David J. *Feedback in Professional Learning Communities: Exploring Teachers' and Administrators' Experiences and Implications for Building Systemic and Sustained Learning.* October 2012. Retrieved from https://conservancy.umn.edu/bitstream/handle/11299/143949/1/Roloff_umn_0130E_13238.pdf.

3. Ullman, Ellen. "How to Create a Professional Learning Community." December 23, 2009. Retrieved from https://www.edutopia.org/professional-learning-communities-collaboration-how-to.

4. "Professional Learning Communities." Public Schools of North Carolina. Retrieved from http://www.dpi.state.nc.us/profdev/resources/proflearn/step4. Accessed June 3, 2018.

5. Coleman, Charlie. "Revitalizing Your PLC." All Things PLC blog. Retrieved from http://www.allthingsplc.info/blog/view/194/revitalizing-your-plc. Accessed June 5, 2018.

2
Gather the Goals

Every professional learning community gathers together the expertise of many people to address issues. The moment the group begins to consider its goals, however, things can suddenly seem overwhelming.

The structure itself is complex. Districts comprise schools, the students and parents who live in the communities, and the staff who might come from different areas to work in the schools. Children of every age and ability level must be served. The needs of teachers and administrators have to be kept in mind.

Deciding where to begin can be like peering into an impenetrable tangle of brush. But the professional learning community has a powerful set of tools: the knowledge of its members. Understanding what each person brings to the group will allow your group to pave a road through the forest along pathways that make logical sense.

THE EDUCATIONAL FOREST

Recognize that your school district is an ecosystem. Its environment is made up of many parts. Some of those elements will change from year to year, while others will remain fairly stable. Your task as a member of a learning community is to view this ecosystem as both a single unit and as its constituent parts.

Begin with the forest itself. As you turn toward goal setting, remember that the initial goals should be broad enough to encompass all the schools in your district.[1] You will likely see that these types of overarching goals initially caused the professional learning group to be formed. Turn to the expertise of your group's members to zero in on critical issues.

Ask why each individual came to the group. Frequently, they know about certain issues faced by their students and peers. Make a list of every issue, even if it appears to be too small to become a broad goal. As your list grows, group together similar issues. Similar issues often point to a deep-seated element that should become a broad PLC goal.

Next, consider how your district compares to other districts in the state. Also compare your district to those nationwide. Is a lower academic rank evident? Are the graduation rates similar to other districts in the state, yet are significantly different from districts in other states? Any differences are areas ripe for exploration.

Generate the same types of comparisons between grade levels, in curricular areas, and other wide-reaching elements. Broad comparisons like these allow the PLC to generate its primary goals. For example, districts typically want to raise academic achievement and/or close the educational gap. These types of broad goals, once they are set, become the foundation for more precise goal setting.

During this step, recognize that every type of goal, from small to large, should be measurable. Abstract desires like spurring lifelong learning are laudable, but they can't be measured during the student's primary education years. Instead, ideals that cannot be monitored find their home in the group's mission statement.

Common broad goals for PLCs include:

- Learning for all: Every student, regardless of their cultural or socioeconomic background, receives the same education.
- Close the education gap: Equalize academic achievement between different groups of students.
- Build a culture of collaboration: Pull in every type of community member from students through administrators to support academic excellence.

FIND THE MICROCLIMATES

Most ecosystems cover a large territory. Different parts can therefore experience different climates. Your school district is probably going to be the same. One school might have lower literacy scores. Several might outperform others in mathematics or science. Each of these unique elements signals that something is different about that school compared to the others.

When you are setting the group's initial goals, you do not need to know why these differences exist. Locating and understanding the causes will come later. For now, you only need to recognize that one school, grade level, or group is different from the rest. Locate them using data gathered during previous academic years, and make a list.

Now that the professional learning community has this data, it is ready to set specific goals. First, focus a spotlight on specific challenges within the schools. Next, recognize areas where each of the schools performs well. When you know what's working well, your group's efforts will avoid changes to elements that don't need to be changed.

Now attention turns to the critical areas that require adjustment. Let's assume that the failure to achieve reading proficiency among fifth graders is a clear and evident problem. Your PLC now has one targeted goal: enhance reading proficiency among fifth graders.

Again, at this point, the cause or causes of the problem are not important. The focus should remain on the issue itself.

With fifth-grade literacy on the table, consider whether the district's ecosystem shows evidence of microclimates related to this challenge. The failure might be more pronounced in one school than the others. The failure might be confined to one or two schools, with the remaining schools outperforming national averages.

All these numbers, good and bad, show that some schools are different. The schools that are different represent a microclimate within your district. By looking closely at the numbers associated with the problem, and by considering the numbers associated with the standard or high-performing groups, you can uncover other differences.

You might, for example, discover that students from the high-performing schools have different socioeconomic backgrounds. The average performers might be clustered in a particular school with a high influx of new teachers. Facility issues can impact achievement, as can community support. Look for differences in every area, not only those associated with test scores, to uncover real-world impacts.

If the PLC takes data for the entire district together, members work with an average. They cannot recognize that some populations or schools are doing just fine while others are lagging. The approach to enhancing reading proficiency among fifth graders might require a different approach in some schools, but not all schools.

By considering whether the district has microclimates and how conditions in those microclimates are different, the PLC takes a huge step forward. Its efforts will target the specific areas that actually need improvement. The fifth graders who are achieving expected levels of reading proficiency can be left alone.

Searching for microclimates enhances the PLC's approach because it focuses on actual problems. It avoids efforts that become scattered because they are too generalized. Taking this extra step while setting goals allows the group to work smarter rather than harder. South Elementary School in Eldon, Missouri, found not only a "phenomenal" impact on teaching and learning, but also experienced "growth as a whole" using a similar approach.[2] Real solutions will lead to real results.

Common specific goals for learning communities include:

- Close educational gaps between/among different groups of students, different schools, and/or their district compared to other districts.
- Target a single grade level across the district, two or more grade levels across the district, or single/multiple grade levels within specific schools.
- Enhance academic achievement in specific curricular topics across the district or within specific schools or grade levels.

SPECIFY THE SPECIES

Your PLC has recognized the district's circumstances and set broad goals related to that ecosystem. The unique elements that set one school or grade level apart from another have been delineated. Keeping both of those elements in mind, the group can determine the species of trees that exist in their forest.

This step generates the list of specific goals for your learning community. Targeted goals will relate exactly to the challenges that have been separated from the primary issues. The broad goal of enhancing fifth-grade reading comprehension rates will be achieved by targeting the schools where fifth graders are struggling.

Note that, at this stage, the PLC still has not considered the reasons behind the poor results. This is entirely appropriate. Setting goals is not the same as defining what needs to be done to achieve those goals. Pinpointing the elements that cause trouble requires a dedicated review of a number of factors. It's impossible to debate every possible weakness before the goal has been set. Save yourself a lot of time and effort by setting the goal before delving into the causes.

At least one meeting at the beginning and end of every school year should focus on goal setting. Rigorous lessons are not enough.[3] Setting goals at the end of the year allows the group to conduct additional research, formulate detailed action plans, and call on resources that might not be accessible during the academic months.

Setting goals at the beginning of the year allows the group to adjust the ones selected at the end of the prior year in the face of new information. Through this avenue, adjustments can be made based on unexpected changes in the district or a single school. Finally, it allows for new ideas to be added to the docket.

Goals that can be set at the end of the year include:

- Conduct new or additional research in critical areas.
- Plan outreach programs that span the summer and midterm breaks.
- Invite other educational professionals to meet with the PLC in an informal setting.

Goals that can be set at the beginning of the year include:

- Set up team-teaching options to help low-performing and new teachers enhance their skills.
- Adjust plans implemented during the previous year to boost results.
- Modify plans associated with one task to fit a similar yet separate task.

HOW DOES YOUR FOREST GROW?

With a thoughtful and specific list of goals in hand, the professional learning community is now ready to determine potential impacts. Sticking with our environmental analogy, you ask, "How does the targeted species grow?"

To answer that, you must determine two things. First determine which elements nurture positive growth. These are the resources and activities that helped achieve similar goals in the past. It is important to recognize these elements so that your learning community can be effective.

Second, and equally important, is to determine potential challenges and obstacles. Note the use of the word "potential." Too often, schools are placed under mandates based on assumptions as much as data. It's perfectly fine to investigate suspected causes of problems. The PLC cannot, however, afford to operate on assumptions that turn out to be false.

The lists of positive and negative elements at this point should be understood to be in the "potential" category. Generate the lists through brainstorming. Brainstorming allows for intuitive knowledge based on experiences rather than data. This ensures that your net is cast as widely as possible. You don't want to miss an issue simply because there's no data available around that challenge.

Once the lists have been generated, your members can determine which are based on facts and which need further research. For the latter, the PLC must commit to proving that these challenges and benefits are real.

For example, outdated computer equipment might be suspected of causing a downturn in science scores. But if the district is using the same equipment that allows other districts to perform well, the group needs to keep digging. Point by point, the list should be culled to only those elements known to be real.

Reduce the list further by merging similar elements. If two grade levels are having issues in the same subject, ask whether the curricula are similar enough to be combined into a single goal. If the issues involve grade levels that are too dissimilar, this won't be an option. But if second and third graders are the target, it might be possible to formulate a single goal.

Tightening up the list helps the PLC stay focused. A shorter list of goals makes the workload more manageable, and it prevents your members from being overwhelmed or burning out. Importantly, it also facilitates communication when your group begins working with other educators and administrators.

Learning communities often tackle issues that are connected to multiple elements. The more your group can simplify and clarify those connections, the greater the support you'll receive from others. And with better support, your PLC can enact the kind of change that results in success.

EMBRACE EXOTICS

Every ecosystem supports a handful of species or individuals that just don't seem to belong. These exotics might have moved there to take advantage of resources that are unavailable in other environments. They might have arrived accidentally.

In any case, they are so different that they stand out. These unusual elements create unique cases that your learning community must recognize and understand.

To address the challenges they present and make use of the opportunities they provide, your group must generate a unique set of goals.

Every learning community will find exotics in their community. A previous example was of one school significantly outperforming other schools in a specific subject. It is very important that your group recognize these types of anomalies. Different groups can present challenges. They can also be rich sources of solutions.

Your goal is to understand how positive impacts can be generated in other areas. Do superior readers have exceptional teachers? Are their classrooms in possession of resources that are not being utilized at other schools? What instructional methods are present or absent compared to standard or low-performing classrooms? With data like this, you can set goals that enhance literacy levels across the board.

Of course, a lot of effort will be dedicated to anomalies that are negative. Begin with the specific challenge your group identified. Then consider the elements that surround the challenge, like resource availability, curricula, and the like. Hone in on components that are not set up as expected or that are being used differently. Target these exotics with your goals.

Always consider the exotics within the professional learning community. These might fall into a variety of areas, especially if your PLC includes administrators, parents, and individuals from outside education. In every case, you're actually locating resources.

Look for positive components like experience resolving issues in other industries. Seek out business-management skills that can be applied to the PLC's operating procedures. Hunt down professional training in learning or socialization. When these skills are directed to certain tasks, your group creates uniquely powerful opportunities for success.

Because every PLC is a group of human beings, be alert for elements that might have a negative impact. Individuals might be well suited to participate in several goals. But if they don't have the ability to participate throughout the timeline of a long-term task, their participation might not be as effective.

Remember that some negative impacts might not be discovered until work begins. Individuals who jump in with both feet only to gradually pull back might have allowed their enthusiasm to override an accurate assessment of what they can actually accomplish. Other members of the PLC should be willing to step in and, armed with considerable compassion, help resolve the issue.

CULTIVATE INDIVIDUAL PLOTS

Part of the PLC's ecosystem includes the staff of the school, the district office, and the school board. The PLC is therefore perfectly positioned to help educational professionals grow. Your group can change perspectives, expand skill sets, and help achieve superior results in the classroom.

Every community will have members at various levels of experience. Each individual will have some areas in which they excel. Early-career teachers will have different goals from mid-career professionals. Even though the abilities and goals are diverse, the strength of the PLC comes from these differences.

Curriculum and instructional issues, for example, can benefit from the wisdom of late-career professionals. The educators with the most experience will benefit from the fresh perspectives and innovative ideas of early- and mid-career teachers. Edutopia points out that this type of collaboration can transform a school system.[4]

When setting individual goals, merge like with like. Find individuals who can lift each other as they work toward the PLC's goals. By paying attention to individual fields, your group will harvest much more.

Remember that the specifics of each goal might appear to be geared toward short-term benefits. In actuality, though, achieving short-term goals generates long-term benefits. An educator who integrates new media formats this year develops skills that will prove valuable for years to come. The teacher who learns how to assist special needs students will be better prepared to work patiently and compassionately with other students.

Every goal, then, works over time to lift the entire population. Nothing your learning community does is ever going to provide a one-off benefit. All of your group's efforts will improve the health of your educational ecosystem.

FOREST MANAGEMENT

By this point, your professional learning community is going to have a lot of ideas about how specific groups, schools, and the entire district can advance. The group will know much more about the ecosystem as a whole and will be aware of the district's microclimates. Unique resources and potential challenges will also be on the radar.

Utilizing the wholeness of this data set, it's time to finalize your goals. Begin by sorting through the list to determine which areas are most critical. Before the list is parsed out into additional categories, take a step back. Ask one key question: Would meeting a less-critical goal help meet a critical goal? If so, pair the two goals on the list.

Now for the second step. Among the critical goals, consider which ones are broad and which are specific. Will meeting one goal first make the path to the other goal easier? If so, pair them on the list.

Next, group together similar goals. For example, if several goals relate to a specific type of resource, separate them into one cluster. Goals that relate to academic performance are separated into a second cluster.

Determine whether the clusters can be subdivided. Some academic performance goals might be specific to actions the PLC will take with parents. Other academic goals might require the PLC to work with teachers. Parse the clusters into subgroups.

By the end, you will have generated several groups of related goals. The team assigned to each goal can determine whether to tackle it as a group or split it across smaller committees. This process of pairing and matching clarifies the job that stands in front of the community. It also makes the job easier to tackle.

SLINGS AND ARROWS (GOAL SHEETS)

For each goal, draw up a list of slings and arrows. *Slings* are things that can propel the group forward toward meeting the goal. *Arrows* are potential challenges that should be targeted.

Use one table, like the example in table 2.1, for each goal. After stating the goal on a blank goal sheet (table 2.4), fill in historical data and other information related to the goal. At the bottom of each chart you'll find "area" and "grade level" slots. These allow the goals to be easily paired.

The bottom box provides room for special circumstances. Here your team can list impacts associated with students, instructors, curricular elements, community conditions, and other unique considerations.

This last box can be very important. The things listed there might indicate that the goals that once seemed similar aren't actually going to be easy to tackle together. The comments can also prepare the group to anticipate unique conditions as their work progresses.

Tables 2.2 and 2.3 provide two more examples of common PLC goals and their associated slings and arrows. Following these examples are the blank tables for your group to use. Photocopy the page, or set up your own table format in a Word file. Use the tables to work through each goal, its history, and the associated slings and arrows.

Goal: Increase the number of students who pass the district common assessment test to 85%.	
Historical Elements and Current Status: Last year, 63% of students passed. Another 12% scored 1 to 3 points below the level needed to pass. This level has been consistent for three years.	
Slings	**Arrows**
Analysis of prior three years of assessment test scores can identify areas of strength and weakness.	Three years of data will require several months to review. Consider reviewing the most recent year's data first so that efforts can begin while additional years are under review.
Courses on district assessment test preparation are available.	The courses on district assessment test preparation do not begin in time for the skills to be applied efficiently. Consider calling on individuals who have taken these courses already.
Pre- and post-assessment test reviews based on learning targets can be drawn up by one member.	

Exit slips can provide formative assessments as often as required to track progress.	
Area: District-wide **Grade level:** N/A **Other special elements:** Target assumes that the 12% failing by only a few points will be pulled up, and that an additional 10% of students failing by more than 3 points will pass.	

Table 2.2

	**Goal:** Third-grade students will improve their math problem-solving skills by 35% as measured in the district assessment test.
	**Historical Elements and Current Status:** Last year, math assessment scores dropped by 3% overall due to exceptionally poor performance in problem solving.
Slings	**Arrows**
Problem solving involves active participation rather than passive learning.	Number stories can be difficult for students with low literacy skills. Consider presenting problems that can be provided in visual and/or tactile formats as well as written forms.
A local nonprofit organization offers free tutoring to elementary school students in STEM subjects.	The nonprofit's tutors require that students be tutored at their facility, but they do not offer transportation from school grounds.
Problem-solving skills in math can easily be integrated as cross-curricular elements in other subjects.	
	**Area:** Mathematics **Grade level:** 3 **Other special elements:** Elementary school students in the district come from families that have difficulty supporting extracurricular activities like tutoring.

Table 2.3

	**Goal:** Generate 70% mastery of vocabulary content for an American history unit.
	**Historical Elements and Current Status:** Last year's unit on this topic failed to achieve this minimum level.
Slings	**Arrows**
The school's writing program offers an opportunity to develop cross-curricular elements.	Few alternative teaching materials exist for this particular time in American history. Consider utilizing novels and movies based on real events to enhance discussions of actual events.
A local history museum is developing a significant display based on this time period.	The display will not be open to the public before the end of the academic year. Consider asking for a behind-the-scenes tour for eleventh-grade students.
	**Area:** American history **Grade level:** 11 **Other special elements:** This goal applies to Randleman High.

These examples have covered district-wide goals, grade-specific goals, and goals that target a specific curricular element within one school. In the "arrows" columns, some potential obstacles have potential solutions included. It is important to allow group members to record their ideas about solutions on the chart. That way, no ideas will be lost as the team moves forward. (A blank chart, table 2.4, is provided on page 29.)

GOAL PROMPTS

This list of goals provides a starting point for your professional learning community. Some of these goals can be immediately adopted by your group with only minor changes. Others will trigger a recognition of similar needs in other curricular areas, grade levels, and the like.

Broad Goals

- Demonstrate proficiency on state assessment tests by 89 percent of students.
- Increase the number of students passing grade levels by 3 percent.
- Increase the college readiness and higher-education awareness of students from elementary through high school.
- Encourage more STEM-career opportunities by engaging more students in extracurricular STEM activities by a minimum 15 percent increase in enrollment.
- All students will show evidence of growth in mathematics by achieving a 5 percent higher score over the previous year's testing.
- Reduce the level of nonproficient students in literacy by 3 percent within every grade level.
- Build strong content knowledge across subject levels by ensuring that students engage with works of quality and substance in all curricular areas.
- Implement classroom activities that enhance engagement for all types of learning styles.
- Introduce digital media and software that thoughtfully enhance the classroom experience.
- Survey curricular areas to ensure that other perspectives are integrated.

Specific Goals

- District standards for the second grade end-of-year writing prompt met by 75 percent of students.
- Improve end-of-trimester summative measures for tenth graders to a 70 percent correct response rate.
- Improve grade-level science skills in middle school classrooms by moving 50 to 75 percent of the students at least one level on the rubric.

- Improve music literacy for students as measured by common vocabulary proficiency of 70 percent or more.
- Improve student attendance at district elementary schools by reducing unexcused absences from 23 days to 5 days.
- Improve inferencing skills among third graders from a baseline of 38 percent to a targeted goal of 74 percent or higher.
- Develop citizenship skills among middle school students by moving them from the current level of 62 percent proficiency to 78 percent proficiency.
- Improve writing skills among students in eleventh grade who display less than 75 percent proficiency.
- Reduce the number of individuals who fail to graduate by 10 percent over the previous academic year.
- Integrate opportunities to provide written textual evidence in science courses in the fifth grade.
- Utilize diverse media and formats so that students can evaluate content visually as well as through text and spoken words.

Unique and Short-Term Goals

- Achieve a 45 percent proficiency rate for music-vocabulary literacy by fall to meet the 70 percent goal by spring.
- Improve executive functioning skills of special education students to 60 percent on average.
- Seventy-eight percent of second graders will be able to use temporal words to explain the sequence of events at the end of the curricular unit.
- Ninth-grade students will demonstrate a 5 percent growth in vocabulary as measured by an increase in the number scoring at high and proficient levels.
- By year's end, ESL students in the fifth grade will improve their vocabulary proficiency by 23 percent.
- Improve reading rates from 70 wcpm (words correct per minute) to 90 wcpm for at-risk second graders.
- For eleventh-grade students receiving a free/reduced lunch, increase the number assessed as proficient by 15 percent.
- Enhance college-level vocabulary in AP classrooms by 5 percent as measured by quarterly testing.
- Improve assessment test results relating to craft and structure reading standards for kindergartners in specific schools by 12 percent.
- Increase average reading and comprehension skills in fourth-grade students to at least 70 percent proficiency among individuals selected for summer tutorial programs before the beginning of their fifth academic year.

PROFESSIONAL LEARNING GOALS FOR MEMBERS

- Improve student engagement by implementing rigor in teaching and by engaging students in multiple learning modalities.
- Generate a learning-style inventory for every student.
- Design lessons that address different learning styles.
- Integrate literacy strategies into instructional methods.
- Engage students in high-level critical thinking through enhanced questioning techniques.
- Provide training in best practices for mentoring new teachers.
- Enhance skills in teaching students with special needs through online training courses and observation of mentor instructors.
- Increase the use of student technology inside the classroom by integrating available technology in additional curricular areas.
- Add online writing tools to classroom procedures to enhance sharing and co-learning opportunities.

NOTES

1. Marczak, Chris. "SMART Goal Setting to Impact Personalized Learning for Students." LEAD Conference, 2013. Retrieved from http://www.artzak.com/plc/SMARTGSLEAD.pdf.

2. Rentfro, Erin. "Professional Learning Communities Impact Student Success." *Leadership Compass*, vol. 5, no. 2, winter 2007. Retrieved from https://www.naesp.org/sites/default/files/resources/2/Leadership_Compass/2007/LC2007v5n2a3.pdf.

3. Weber, Steven. "Five Dysfunctions of a Professional Learning Community." *The Whole Child* (blog), October 26, 2011. Retrieved from http://www.wholechildeducation.org/blog/five-dysfunctions-of-a-professional-learning-community.

4. Ullman, Ellen. "Teachers and Community Members Practice TLC with PLCs." *Edutopia*, December 23, 2009. Retrieved from https://www.edutopia.org/professional-learning-communities-collaboration.

Table 2.4

Goal:	
Historical Elements and Current Status:	

Slings	Arrows

Area:

Grade level:

Other special elements:

3
Going Live

A professional learning community expends effort during meetings, while conducting research, and while providing training. To capitalize on that work, your group's recommendations must be integrated in the classroom. Theoretical structures, discussion, and debate can open a variety of new channels. At some point, those channels must lead directly into the schools.

A careful approach is required. When enthusiasm overtakes effective methods, the results can be disastrous. Your learning community must wisely select the specific ideas and programs it will implement. Just as critically, your group must determine which grades, schools, and teachers are the best targets for each task.

That sounds like an awfully tall order. Really, though, the same dynamics that brought the PLC together will lead them through this stage. Experienced professionals who utilize their instinct and combine their breadth of knowledge always find the best way forward.

BEGIN AT THE BEGINNING

Every time your PLC must decide how to transition from ideas into practice, return to the beginning. The core component of your mission will always be academic achievement. From that single point, consider what students should learn.

Your goal might involve a specific skill, a certain unit, or cross-curricular abilities. While reaching for the goal, your group must also ensure compliance with state and federal guidelines and requirements. Therefore, use relevant portions of the regulations as your starting point.

Have the group agree on the specific goal or goals, and write them down. These essential outcomes will set the stage for growth in the current year. They will also be targets that guide increasing levels of success for the school community in the future.

Finally—and this one is really important—consider whether any of the PLC's other goals have connection points. Some connecting points will be fairly obvious, as is the case when several goals target a single grade or an individual school. You already took one step to merge goals. Now you'll look again to see whether you recognize additional tie-ins.

The second look is necessary because conditions change. By the time you've moved from setting the goal to being able to implement the goal, additional areas of repetition might have emerged. Taking this one time-out to consider newly developed connecting points will streamline your efforts.

Some overlapping areas won't be obvious. Subtle tie-ins might include things like the use of similar (or the same) resources for widely variable goals. The PLC should avoid placing too many demands on a single resource, especially if the resource is limited.

Resources include the people on the PLC team and in the community. Recognizing that multiple goals will draw from the same talent pool will allow the group to plan more effectively. Whenever possible, merge tasks so that a single meeting with a community resource serves two tasks. Ask a professional to train a group member in a particular skill so that a single visit provides skills for the group.

Setting schedules so that resources can overlap or be used fully by one team at a time maximizes your overall chances for success. It prevents resources from becoming exhausted too soon, and sends the most resources to the most critical areas.

PLANNING FOR SUCCESS

Now it's time to break the entire learning community group into smaller task forces called planning teams. Assign one planning team to each of the PLC's goals. Since you already recognize areas where connections occur, you can assign one individual to two or more overlapping teams.

In addition to using a single resource for multiple teams, splitting resources this way provides other benefits. When persons have a working knowledge of the efforts going on across more than one team, they have a bigger perspective on other efforts that could be combined. The efficiency and effectiveness of your efforts automatically increase.

Once the planning teams are defined, each team should consider its goal and its essential outcomes. Determine the resources, including people, that will be required. Recognize that most goals have different stages. Each stage might require different sets of resources. Does the planning team have everything and everyone needed throughout the project?

Once you know what resources will be required, write them down. Now compare the essential outcomes to the resource list. Will the effort involved in the project stay the same or will efforts grow over time? Answering this question will alert the group to the need for more resources or different resources at future milestones.

Have the planning team consider which evidence-based instructional strategies will meet the standards. Select the instructional strategy that can be implemented using only the available resources. Don't go down a road hoping to find resources later. Get them now, or find another way forward.

At this point, a two-pronged approach will forge the best pathway. One prong encompasses the team's experience. The other sparks the team's creativity.

Mine the team's experiences to determine which approaches have met with success in the past. Real-world events will tell you what worked well. They will also reveal the components that didn't serve as well as they should have. Make whatever adjustments are required to generate an approach that meets the goals.

Creativity is the second prong. This option can lead the way to ingenious new ideas. Ask your planning team whether available resources can be used differently to maximize results. Can existing resources be combined in new ways to enhance productivity or efficiency?

The idea is to open the gateway to new ideas. The top resource of every school and professional learning community is its people. The human mind can come up with unique options. When the box is too confining, thinking outside the box leads to greater success.

DEVELOP THE PROGRAM

Often, the PLC's planning teams will develop a common lesson plan that meets the stated goal or goals. The plan will incorporate selected strategies and will identify the type of work students will perform. When the goal of one team connects with those of a different team, they can share drafts of their lesson plans to help each other advance more quickly.

Each lesson plan should mark the work and work products that will demonstrate learning. The ways in which students move toward the goals should include multiple learning methodologies. Additional considerations can be made for special learners who are part of the target population.

The plan should include the steps teachers will take to gather evidence of learning. Testing should only be one piece of this aspect. Include different markers like participation rates, completion rates, and speed of individual advances. A variety of measures will pinpoint the strengths and weaknesses in the lesson plan.

For additional data that can be quite meaningful, include opportunities for students to provide feedback. What part of the lesson plan sparked their interest the most? Where did they struggle to understand the assignments? Did they feel that the information could have been presented in a different medium or format?

The best PLCs recognize that the entire community, including the students, should be included in the learning process. From a surprisingly early age, students can become proactive learners. Giving them the opportunity to sound off about lesson plans, curricular units, and presentation formats can provide useful information.

TEACHER PORTFOLIOS

Student portfolios are a fairly common way to evaluate coursework, individual progress, and academic achievement. They also provide a comprehensive and easy method for students to assess their own progress. Over time, these portfolios become a rich resource that can be utilized by students, parents, and educators.

The same is true when teachers generate portfolios to track their progress with PLC initiatives. They become a focal point for the reflective process that determines how well a teaching goal has been met. And since they can be shared with others, a teacher's portfolio can implement change in other classrooms.

This is truly one of the learning community's shining moments. By compiling real evidence, anecdotes, and thoughts as they occur, the teacher portfolio becomes a guiding light. It can take the guesswork out of an individual's approach to implementing the lesson plan in their classroom.

Importantly, portfolios generated across multiple classrooms and grade levels can be combined. From this compiled information, a variety of best practices can be extracted and shared. Since these recommendations are about current efforts within the school community, they are infinitely more valuable than pages of tips culled from other sources.

For these reasons, PLCs should encourage educators to create teacher portfolios. Since many learning community programs are multiyear efforts, seeing how portfolios and experiences change from one year to the next can reveal which adjustments should be made over time.

The portfolios become living documents that grow and change along with the students and the schools. As such, they will be harbingers of shifts that might otherwise go unnoticed. Things like economic downturns that make learning more difficult can be caught early enough in the year for teachers to respond.

Any insights garnered from teacher portfolios should be shared anonymously. Questions about specific ideas or anecdotes can be directed to the learning community. The group's members can formulate a response without having to return to the source. This nurtures the trust that teachers place in the PLC when they share their portfolios.

Individuals might be open to responding directly. This can be handled by asking individuals to monitor and post to a message board. Allowing for this free exchange of information extends the trust even further. Anyone who opts not to respond as an individual is still secure in the knowledge that their reflections remain anonymous.

Through this approach, the wisdom of the entire district can be tapped. Nancy Krakowka, who teaches sixth-grade language arts and social studies, knows how much the information she shares can help her school.

"When I started," she said, "I was very protective of my curriculum. But some of my colleagues have better ideas than I do. When you put all these minds together, the end product comes out much better."[1]

CALL ON THE COMMUNITY

Some professional learning communities are made up mostly of teachers. This is acceptable because their experiences usually cover a variety of areas. Often, too, the dynamic allows educators to be entirely honest while discussing goals and issues at their schools.

When the time comes for the PLC's plans to be implemented in the classroom, however, this kind of group might do much better if they reach out to others. Richard DuFour, an education consultant who specializes in creating PLCs, says, "we need to work collectively to help everyone be successful."[2] And that includes inviting individuals from across the community to participate in every initiative.

Each school's community is made up of a wide diversity of people. Families of every type are impacted by the activities that take place inside schools. Parents who want to be more proactive can get involved in short-term efforts. Individuals who have seen their adult children leave home can participate where they are needed most.

Drawing on the community expands your learning community's experience base. With only educational professionals in the room, new advances in technology might be overlooked. People from the community might know about the perfect low-cost app or device. If your group relies only on educators, you might overlook solutions.

The time to reach out to the larger community is when the planning teams are created. Use public service announcements at local radio stations, free listings in newspapers, and social media to find individuals who can help. Even if they only step in for a short time, their participation could prove to be invaluable.

PERSONALIZE IMPLEMENTATION

Once the program has been planned and created, one more step is required before it can be implemented in the classroom. The plan must be personalized. The resources, steps, and approach should be adjusted so that each teacher can serve every student's specific needs.

Nowadays, educational professionals recognize that students come from a variety of backgrounds and cultures. Individual learners also display unique learning preferences, skill levels, academic ability, and other factors. Educators must reach them where they stand to maximize educational achievement.

The same is true for the teachers who lead those classrooms. Two individuals can attend the same college, achieve the same grades in the same courses, and graduate on the same day. And yet they will still be as different in their approach, their skill levels, and their teaching preferences as two individuals separated by generation or geography.

Your learning community is in an excellent position to help every educator discover the best way to implement the group's initiates. In fact, the PLC should work with teachers in this area as the programs are developed. By building the programs with the teachers in mind, educators gain confidence in their ability to implement the PLC's programs.

The finished programs can then be modified in granular ways to meet the needs of various learning groups. ESL students, for example, will trigger a different set of adjustments than a classroom with developmentally disabled students. By considering the instructor at one stage and the students at a different stage, the program is tailor-made to fit every need.

This approach has important additional advantages. In addition to building the educator's confidence, the connections made while the program is adapted open communication. These channels can be important to the program's success, so building them up front makes sense.

Another advantage is that the process of making adjustments smooths the process. Programs that consider the needs of both educational professionals and students can be integrated more easily. Efforts that normally would fall to the teacher can be shared with one or more members of the learning community. Buy-in soars, and success increases.

The advantages run both ways. By working with specific individuals and considering specific learning groups, the PLC discovers ways to improve their approach. Since these improvements can be woven into the program before it goes live, effectiveness and efficiency are maximized.

Greater academic achievement, the learning community's primary goal, is the result. Personalized implementation is therefore a must. When your PLC takes the lead in adjusting the programs, your efforts are met with open arms. Everyone benefits.

COLLEGIAL IMPLEMENTATION

The professional learning community's approach hinges on harmonious and interdependent effort. In this kind of system, no educator, parent, or student stands alone. Everyone in the district works together to achieve common goals.

Never is this more evident than when implementing a PLC program. The learning community has generated a plan or program with the assistance of the larger community. When the program enters the classroom, the same community ties enhance the chances for success.

The principal guides the school in implementing the PLC's recommendations. When issues arise, the staff work together to brainstorm solutions that fit their school's environment. Colleagues of the teachers involved with the program can see, on a day to day basis, how students are transforming.

As the other teachers compare their students to those of their peers, they become more receptive to change. They want their students to become active participants in the learning community's efforts. They become volunteers and champions of the PLC's programs.

John Hattie, a professor and educational researcher, reviewed more than 800 meta-analyses that sampled a total of over 80 million students.[3] In determining what works best in education, he found that teachers should be organized into collaborative teams.

In other words, all schools should become professional learning communities. The results are that powerful.

RETURN TO THE BEGINNING

As the professional learning community prepares to implement their efforts in classrooms, return to the group's core mission statement. Consider all the aspects of the specific goal using the prompts listed below.

Exactly what do we expect students to learn?
_____
_____

What milestones will be reached by each student during their educational journey?
_____
_____

How will we know when each student has achieved each milestone?
_____
_____

For individuals who have difficulty reaching each milestone, what steps will be taken to aid their success?
_____
_____

How will we know when each student has achieved each learning goal?
_____
_____

For individuals who have difficulty reaching the learning goal, what steps will be taken to aid their success?
_____
_____
_____

How will achieving the learning goal mesh with the rest of the curriculum?
_____
_____
_____

How will achieving the learning goal mesh with cross-curricular elements?
_____
_____
_____

LINK THE CONNECTION POINTS

Identifying how the PLC's goals connect will enhance their implementation in the classroom. Any time a connection point is discovered, the individual planning teams can work together to combine resources and reduce overall effort. Use these prompts as a starting point to locate overlapping areas before implementation efforts begin.

Will more than one of the PLC's goals impact the same school, grade level, or curricular topics?
_____
_____
_____

Which cross-curricular efforts already in place can be harnessed to help achieve the PLC's goal?
_____
_____
_____

Will different goals require the use of the same set of resources?
_____
_____
_____

Which teachers, parents, or other human resources can be called on to help each planning team?
_____
_____
_____

If the same set of resources or people will be called on for more than one planning team, how can program schedules or the use of those resources be coordinated?
_____
_____
_____

Does the community have access to organizations outside of public education that can be called on?

What resources can each organization outside of public education offer?

Which other schools or districts have implemented plans that have successfully addressed the same or similar goals?

What lessons can be learned from similar efforts conducted by other PLCs, schools, or districts?

Can resources that are not depleted by use (such as equipment) be borrowed from other schools or districts?

TEAM GOALS

Each team should list the specific goals embedded in their program. These goals should include the milestones that can be measured as progress is made. The prompts listed here will help chart the course to be taken inside the classroom.

Essential Outcomes

Which outcomes are essential to successfully achieving the goal?

When should these essential outcomes be met in the academic year?

How will teachers recognize when these essential outcomes are met?

What resources are already on hand to help meet this outcome?

What resources are needed for the team to meet this outcome?

Milestone Achievements

Which specific milestone achievements should teachers work toward?

When should each milestone be achieved in the academic year?

How will teachers recognize when each milestone has been achieved?

What resources are already on hand to help achieve each milestone?

What resources are needed for each milestone?

Comparison Points

Which resources are required to meet the essential outcome?

Which resources are required to meet specific milestones?

How can the overlapping needs be managed?

Table 3.1 has a blank form for resources and overlapping areas.

Table 3.1   RESOURCE LIST

Resource	Required for Essential Outcome (Y/N)	Required for Milestones (Y/N)	In Hand? (Y/N)	Potential Source
People				
Organizations				
Community				
Equipment/Other				

LESSON PLAN TEMPLATE

Date: ─────────────────────────────────
Grade/class: ─────────────────────────────────
Topic: ─────────────────────────────────
Instructional objective/s:
_____
_____
_____

Essential knowledge and skills:
_____
_____
_____

Materials/equipment needed:
_____
_____
_____

Focus question/activity/demonstration/introduction:
_____
_____
_____

Generating questions:
_____
_____
_____

Activity/procedure for students to perform:
_____
_____
_____

Data to be gathered/areas to be considered:
_____
_____
_____

Interpretation and conclusion:
_____
_____
_____

Assessment areas/evidence teacher will gather of student learning:
_____
_____
_____

STUDENT FEEDBACK

What area of today's lesson was most interesting to you?
___
___

Were any of the instructions confusing?
___
___

Which parts of the lesson were the hardest to complete?
___
___

What would have helped you complete the lesson?
___
___

Were the handouts/video/tables easy to understand?
___
___

If you were teaching this lesson to your friend, how would you help them learn?
___
___

PORTFOLIO TIPS

Have teachers start their portfolios early. Individuals can decide what to include as the year progresses. When the portfolios are kept throughout the year, the work flow of each individual is right at hand.

Determine the overarching goal of the portfolio. Portfolios can be kept to determine how much a teacher advances professionally during the year. Success or failure in achieving milestones can more easily be determined by reviewing work at the end of each month or between semesters. Reviews can also locate weaknesses in teaching methods or the approach to a curricular topic.

Include multiple items. Portfolios can compile changes in methodologies, fluctuations in grade averages, and reflections on professional learning opportunities. Notes about projects undertaken outside the school, like learning opportunities pursued in nonacademic environments, can be added. Discussions can open communication channels between teachers and the PLC.

Regularly review the portfolios. Schedule this when teachers can get together to review each other's portfolios. When they consider their efforts through the eyes of their peers, they are encouraged by the advancements they have made. The professional interaction allows the group and the individuals to find better ways to achieve academic success.

PERSONALIZE THE PLAN

The planning team should reach out to teachers who will be using the PLC's lesson plans. During this conversation, teachers can share details about the makeup of their classroom. Individuals with special needs can be considered, the educator's skill set can be laid out, and the plan can be adapted. Use these prompts to guide the conversation and launch the entire classroom on the path to success.

What level of ability does the classroom demonstrate compared to the learning goals?
_____
_____

What special educational needs are present in the class?
_____
_____

What resources will the teacher need to achieve the stated goals?
_____
_____

Which teaching preferences will instruction utilize?
_____
_____

Is the community or an individual family experiencing stressors that might impair achievement?
_____
_____

How well are state mandates already being met by this particular class?
_____
_____

Which remedies can the PLC offer to bring the class in line with state mandates?
_____
_____
_____

NOTES

1. Ullman, Ellen. "Teachers and Community Members Practice TLC with PLCs." Edutopia, December 23, 2009. Retrieved from https://www.edutopia.org/professional-learning-communities-collaboration.

2. Ibid.

3. DuFour, Rick. "Professional Learning Communities: The Key to Improved Teaching and Learning." Retrieved from http://www.advanc-ed.org/source/professional-learning-communities-key-improved-teaching-and-learning. Accessed June 5, 2018.

4
Assess and Adapt

Since you're reading this book, you already recognize how valuable a professional learning community can be for a school and district. As you move forward, it's critical to schedule regular assessments of the results your efforts have garnered.

The reasons for this are many. First, you want to ensure that the plans created by your group are pointing students in the right direction. Second, the effectiveness of how those plans are implemented can identify approaches with high success rates. You'll also target those that are weak and be able to make adjustments.

Your PLC will also want to gather measurable data. This information will enhance future efforts by each planning team. You'll be able to pinpoint which elements really work. Interventions can be planned for classrooms that aren't faring well. The same data will be useful to the teachers who guide their students through the programs.

Finally, assessments are the only way to truly determine which areas need to change. The knowledge gathered from these intermittent checks will allow adaptations to occur early enough to ward off larger problems down the road. You'll head into the next academic year with a broader experiential basis.

HOW MANY AND HOW OFTEN

When a PLC first starts operating in a school or district, the group must address concerns from teachers and administrative staff. Educators will want to know which resources are available as well as how the learning community can help locate those resources. This is particularly true when broaching assessments for the first time.

Richard DuFour, an educator turned educational consultant, talked about this in a blog entry he wrote for All Things PLC.[1] When he recommended that teachers implement assessments on a regular schedule, he got some pushback. Educators felt that too many assessments were already being performed. The addition to the workload seemed overwhelming.

He responded by pointing out two important facts. One was that the total number of assessments did not have to be increased. Instead teachers could, and even should, replace some of the existing assessments with the new ones.

Second, and perhaps most important, was that a PLC's assessments are far more powerful than traditional ones. This is true because the entirety of the learning community's focus is on needs that exist on the ground. The previous chapter in this book made that clear by opening communications with educators early in each program's development.

The bottom line is that every student matters to a learning community. Therefore, every student's individual learning needs can be met with your PLC's programs. Assessments are one way to ensure that no student ever misses out on the benefits your group offers.

When you are deciding which existing assessments to eliminate, target those that do not function well for the student populations you serve. Replace them with something tailored to the needs, background, and goals of each school's population.

Keep an eye out for opportunities where one tailored assessment can replace two or more standardized ones. You might be surprised at how often this can happen; the learning community has a broader perspective and often can eliminate overlapping efforts like these. When you do, be sure that everyone knows about it. You'll get far more support when educators have proof of the benefits your PLC is generating.

Once you've come up with a set of assessments that makes sense for your district's needs, set a manageable schedule. In the early years, your learning community might recommend a certain number of assessments spread equally over the year. Once the teachers and administration get used to them, the assessments can be adjusted to better fit curricular needs.

Finally, educators should know that the assessments are flexible. Your learning community is intended to be responsive to their needs. While your advice and assistance should remain available, your group should also signal that teachers lead their own classrooms. They'll be empowered on their own and know that help is available when they decide they need it.

ASSESSING THE DATA

In an article for *The Principalship*, Rick DuFour and Mike Mattos discussed the most effective ways for principals to support learning outcomes.[2] Their message, founded on studies conducted by top educational groups, was that the professional learning community is the key. Part of the reason PLCs can be so powerful is that their toolbox includes tailored assessments.

Assessments should consider the critical areas associated with student learning. Academic achievement is supported by casting a wide assessment net. Students who require more attention should of course be located. Teachers who need more help guiding their classrooms through the academic process will also be discovered.

Assessments will also measure elements at the other end of the spectrum. Individual learners who already demonstrate proficiency with the curriculum can be directed toward opportunities that broaden their scope of learning. The practices of teachers who consistently lift their classrooms above the average can be shared among educators.

Assessments will also reveal flaws in the approach the learning community has taken to achieve its goals. When the desired results aren't met, the PLC must consider its plans. Are the goals that have been set unrealistic? Have the proper resources been made available? Does the PLC need a more diverse group to meet specific needs?

A different type of flaw might be revealed through exceptional success rates. If every classroom and school exceeds the PLC's goals, then students require more of a challenge. By working within the system the learning community has created, your group will seize the opportunity to raise the bar higher. When the schools succeed in reaching these new goals, the PLC will have achieved true and lasting success.

Assess every aspect of learning. Review lesson plans and class assessments. Examine student work samples and performance data. Determine whether the professional literature made available in your schools fits the needs of your educators and learners. Regular consideration of these elements ensures that your schools are constantly meeting students where they stand.

In a very real way, assessments measure the effectiveness of the collaborative culture. The responsibility for student learning is not borne only by the teachers. The professional learning community has taken much of that burden on themselves. Their position provides an overview of the entire school or district. They are therefore the ones best able to knit together a real community by opening new channels to academic achievement.

A SUPPORTIVE APPROACH

Several times before the assessment phase, the PLC sets its own goals in planning sessions. Teachers adopt those goals in ways that are tailored to the needs of their students. When assessments begin, be sure that group goalsetting is one way your learning community judges progress.

Group goalsetting generates powerful results. When members of a group shift from individual goals to a community goal, every person in that community is more likely to achieve success. For PLC efforts, that means a group of teachers sets a common goal within their curricular area.

Efforts to raise the math skills of one group of students (an individual classroom goal) becomes a group effort to raise the math skills of a specific type of learner (developmentally challenged students, for example). The obvious benefit is that more students are helped. What might not be obvious is how this helps educators.

By spotlighting group efforts, PLCs shift the focus of assessments away from teacher performance. Instead, the real goal of every professional learning community, student learning, is in the foreground. Teachers feel safe knowing that any guidance from the PLC is intended to achieve that singular goal. They become more willing to ask for help from their peers as well as the larger community.

This approach has other benefits, as well. It naturally nurtures the instructional leaders who provide exceptional benefits to your schools. Teachers who feel supported will take the initiative to reach out to your learning community for even more opportunities.

ASSESSMENT FOUNDATION

Assessments should be data driven, measurable, and efficient. How these three elements are integrated into your assessments will depend on factors such as curricular topic, grade level, current academic achievement, and the learning community's goals.

Several key elements should always be part of the assessments. First among these is the demographics of the student population. Include participation rates, attendance, and the number of individuals with special needs. This information provides an overview of the group or groups being served by the learning community.[3]

Second, gather data related to learning. Mark the level of knowledge and skills as they relate to your state's standards. Consider where each grade level falls for adequate yearly progress in reading/English language arts and mathematics. Then pull in the prior year's data from standard assessments and test scores.

This collection of academic information will provide a snapshot of the current year's challenges and strengths. Using this picture, your learning community will be able to assess whether the goals are right on target or whether they need to be adjusted. Your group will also be able to adapt tools and resources to the needs of the teachers.

The third key element is disciplinary statistics. Consider whether office referrals or suspensions are being generated in trends that can be identified. Pay attention to potential patterns. This data can reach beyond whether one school or classroom is experiencing turmoil to reflect wider elements.

Community issues often have a negative impact on disciplinary statistics. Families experiencing financial issues, for example, might not be able to provide their children with everything they need to excel. A PLC can lead the outreach to nonprofits that can fill in gaps through charitable contributions or compassionate intervention.

Once your learning group has all the information in hand, look for differences. How are the grade levels that are on track to meet yearly progress goals different from those that are not quite achieving as expected? Locate potential challenges and strengths in every curricular area. Target the weaknesses using the best resources available.

No matter which type of assessment is used, it should be rigorous. It can be performance based, use self-assessments generated by teachers and students, or involve a blended approach. Authentic assessments generate reliable data your group can trust.

TYPES OF ASSESSMENTS

A variety of assessments are available for use by your PLC. The ones that most people are familiar with are summative in nature. The ones that are used most often, however, are formative.[4] In this section, we'll discuss both kinds.

Summative assessments consider, or "sum up," various types of data. When completed, they provide insights to be developed and allow conclusions to be made. Summative assessments are useful for locating at-risk populations, monitoring growth, and ranking how well milestones were achieved.

Most schools already utilize a number of summative assessments. Testing performed to determine proficiency, standardized achievements tests, and state or federally mandated testing are the most common. All are intended to monitor educational outcomes.

Formative assessments, on the other hand, are performed with the learning process in mind. They provide the kind of information that allows teachers (and professional learning groups) to modify classroom activities. Formative assessments are powerful tools for achieving the best academic outcomes.

These types of assessments also provide the widest range of types. The variety makes them immensely helpful. They can be applied to a broad array of topics, and they can be formal or informal. Some require practically zero resources to implement.

A teacher who checks on whether her entire classroom has understood a particular point is conducting an assessment. An administrator who uses annual test scores to develop enrichment training is performing a formative assessment. Students conduct formative assessments when they rank their progress toward a given goal.

In every case, the purpose is to create effective teaching methods. Formative assessments focus on practices while offering equal weight to learner experiences.[5] They reveal what students already know. They empower teachers to modify their instructional approach, and they guide the creation of lesson plans.

When considering which assessments to use, consider the student population. The type of assessments that work for a second-grade reading class might not work as well in a tenth-grade classroom. By the same token, assessments generated to probe results in one school might not work in schools located only a few miles away.

Create a different group of assessments for different goals, schools, and even different classrooms. A fine-grained approach will serve all the students in your district. To support the effort, develop a database of examples and resources. Each planning team can then use and adapt existing materials as needed.

BUILDING THE FORMATIVE ASSESSMENT

Because formative assessments offer so many benefits, the learning community should generate foundational assessments that can be adjusted by individual teachers. The best ones rely on descriptive feedback, appropriate rubrics, and self-assessment. Blending these elements supports ongoing growth.

Each assessment must be founded on the learning goals identified by the PLC. Every assessment must target the enhancement of student learning. This doesn't mean the assessments are always about the students. While they can be used to measure learning, their primary purpose is to enhance learning growth.

Sharing the feedback gathered by assessments should be scheduled in a timely manner. Allow enough time for adaptations to be made to learning community programs during the academic year. At the end of the year, use new data to help set the course for the next year.

Because formative assessments are dynamic, they are useful diagnostic tools. Teachers can adjust lesson plans, their approach, and other classroom elements using data gathered from the previous year. Teachers can also expand their existing plans during the academic year as the need for change becomes clear.

The best part about formative assessments is that they can be used to reach individual learners. When low-performing students and individuals who are struggling are identified, additional time and attention can be dedicated to their needs. High performers and students who easily grasp the curriculum can receive extensions that allow them to go further.

Each PLC planning team should develop assessments that exhibit a clear purpose, focus on specific targets, and provide for effective communication. As the teams work with educators to adapt the assessments, the resulting tools should demonstrate the same key elements.

Typically, formative assessments target four areas. These are knowledge, or the grasp of the subject matter; reasoning, the application of knowledge; skills as demonstrated by observed performance; and tangible products that demonstrate learning.[6]

Assessments can achieve these ends through a variety of means. Valid pathways include selecting a correct response from various options, writing an original short essay in response to a question, performing a skill or creating a specific product, and discussion. A blend of approaches will ensure that individuals with different preferences can be fully and properly measured.

AVOID ASSESSMENT BIAS

As David Wees noted on the Reflective Educator blog, "Every form of assessment of learning has bias."[7] As your learning community sets up new assessment tools and adjusts existing assessments, you will need to minimize bias to the largest degree possible. Awareness of the different types of bias will help you build stronger tools.

One common bias springs from language. Individuals use language in a way that is strongly tied to their personal experience. The very words used to generate an assessment are therefore going to be biased toward how the individual creating the assessment understands language.

The assessment's delivery method can introduce a different type of bias. Individuals who are expected to use unfamiliar electronic devices might struggle with the technology. Capturing any challenges they have with the topic is doubly difficult under these circumstances. The workload is doubled, and accurate information becomes much more difficult to obtain.

Biases can also arise from cultural and socioeconomic differences. Most educators these days are well aware of how one student's background might differ from that of other students. They also know that their own life experiences might be very different from those of their students.

Awareness of these differences goes a long way to eliminating cultural and socioeconomic bias. Educators who are aware of the gaps find ways to reach across those gaps. They can then assess students in ways that are fair.

Fortunately, the professional learning community is in the right position to help. Consider which cultural biases might exist between the pool of professionals working with students and the students themselves. Keep an eye out for gender bias that creeps in because some cultures don't encourage girls to take leadership roles. Stay alert to needs arising from socioeconomic factors and for second-language learners.

In the *Journal of Education,* Teresa Scotton Williams notes that some schools champion nonverbal test forms.[8] This is especially true in the cases of early childhood learners and those being tested for gifted and talented programs. Consider whether this kind of approach might be useful for your assessment tools.

Once a planning team has finished creating or adjusting an assessment, pass it to a different planning team. Ask them to review the assessment for cultural sensitivity, respect for diversity, and a fair representation of gender fluidity. The fresh eyes should also check that the content is accessible to individuals from all socioeconomic strata. Your PLC will ensure that every assessment is fair to every learner.

ANALYZE AND ASSESS: PROMPTS FOR DATA COLLECTION

Use these prompts when reviewing data collected for assessments of the PLC's effectiveness. As a bonus, the same answers can uncover areas that need further attention in the student population.

Is the school/grade/classroom consistently achieving adequate progress year by year?

Has the school/grade/classroom plateaued in how well it performs every year?

If a drop has occurred in advancement or achievement, is the reduction significant enough to require intervention?

If the drop is significant enough to require intervention, was the same trend noted in previous academic years?

What are some possible causes for the drop?

What are some possible solutions to bring the school/grade/classroom back on track?

What resources will be needed to implement these changes?

How can the teacher/s best be supported in this process?

COMMON FORMATIVE ASSESSMENTS

- Brainstorming activities that reveal what students already know.
- Portfolios that document student work.

- Documentation of student conferences that assess individual needs.
- Self-evaluations conducted by students.
- Asking students to assess each other's work.
- Questioning student answers in a way that promotes discussion.
- Discovering how students apply problem-solving skills.
- Ensuring that students understand the learning goals.
- Feeding information back to students in new ways to help them grasp the concept.
- Activities modeled on real-life situations.
- Generative activities in which students discover a new pathway to produce a similar outcome.

SUMMATIVE ASSESSMENT TIPS

Summative assessments encompass any test, assignment, or project designed to measure learning. They:

- Determine whether students have achieved learning goals.
- Determine how well students have achieved learning goals.
- Are often performed at the end of a specific instructional period.
- Are often recorded as scores or grades that factor into the student's academic record.
- Are frequently a major component of the district's grading process.
- Are used to help determine the effectiveness of programs or curriculum.
- Measure progress toward improvement goals.

Summative assessments include:

- Standardized tests for school accountability administered by the state
- End-of-unit/chapter tests
- End-of-term or end-of-semester tests
- Standardized tests used for college admission
- Capstone projects students work on over time
- Demonstrations of learning
- Interim or benchmark testing implemented by a school or district

ASSESS THE ASSESSMENT

Once the planning team has generated its foundational assessments, check each for these key elements.

1. **Content Validity.** Does the assessment actually measure what it is intended to measure? Does the assessment measure only that target and none other? Is the content appropriate for the experiential level the assessment is attempting to measure?
2. **Clarity.** Does the assessment have a clearly defined purpose? Are the educators who will use the assessment aware of this purpose?
3. **Fairness.** Is the assessment free of bias in terms of language used? Will the assessment be unbiased by the format or media in which it will be used? Will individuals from diverse backgrounds be accurately assessed using this tool?
4. **Consistency of Results.** Will the assessment provide consistent results in different situations? Will retesting with the same assessment generate equivalent information?
5. **Use of Results.** Will this assessment provide results that will be useful in enhancing academic performance? At which points should this assessment be used? Will the assessment provide information that is useful in the short term, the long term, or both?

PLC ASSESSMENT FOR SCHOOLS

Use this form to create a survey that allows your professional learning group to consider how their efforts are impacting each school. The questions and the type of ranking you use might change a little or a lot from year to year or from classroom to classroom. Generally, however, this sheet gives you a strong basis to build upon.

At key points in the year, ask all educators involved with your PLC's efforts to respond to the statements listed below using a rank of 1 to 5 where 1 is "not at all" and 5 is "exceptionally well."

___1. The professional learning group's efforts are directly related to learning goals.
___2. All team members demonstrate consensus with the stated targets.
___3. If the PLC did not exist, my students/school/district would suffer.
___4. The attainment of academic achievement has improved as a result of the professional learning group's efforts.
___5. My classroom/school/district has improved as a result of the professional learning group.
___6. The professional learning group is aware of and understands conditions inside the classroom/school/district.
___7. The professional learning group has targeted the most important learning goals for my grade/school/district.
___8. The professional learning group is approachable and accessible.
___9. The professional learning group responds in a timely manner to issues inside the classroom/school/district.

___10. The professional learning group provides resources that are valuable and useful.
___11. My concerns are treated with respect by every member of the professional learning group.
___12. My approach to education has benefited from assistance provided by the professional learning group.
___13. Over the course of this grading period/academic year, the professional learning group has helped with at least one academic issue in my classroom/school/district.
___14. As a professional educator, I find the professional learning group to be capable and trustworthy.
___15. Overall, I feel that the professional learning group's involvement in my classroom/school/district is worth the time and effort.

PLC ASSESSMENT FOR MEMBERS

Self-assessment is as valuable for your learning community as it is for teachers and students. This sheet gives you a starting point for creating a touchstone assessment. Plan to have the group fill out the survey at the end of each term or more frequently.

For these questions, rank answers from 1 to 4 with 1 meaning "strongly agree" and 4 meaning "strongly disagree."

___1. Our group adheres to the norms agreed upon for PLC meetings.
___2. The norms agreed upon help us be more productive and effective.
___3. Each member has clearly designated tasks to perform.
___4. The tasks assigned to each member clearly relate to student learning goals.
___5. Each member shares an equal burden of assigned tasks.
___6. Each member is contributing equally to reaching the PLC's goals.
___7. When disagreements arise, the PLC explores the disagreement in depth and with respect.
___8. All members appear dedicated to the PLC's goals.
___9. I feel highly motivated to achieve the PLC's goals.
___10. My grade/school/district has improved as a result of my learning community's work.
___11. My team regularly administers common assessments to the classrooms/grades they are assigned to assist.
___12. My team uses rubrics to score common assessments.
___13. The rubrics used by my team continue to be effective and efficient.
___14. My team meets regularly to consider adjustments to our approach.
___15. My team meets regularly to consider recommendations/adjustments to instructional practices.

___16. My team has implemented academic interventions for students who are low performers or who are not on track to meet the learning goals.
___17. My team has located resources that can extend the achievement of high performers and those who easily meet learning goals.
___18. My team notes instructional practices that seem most effective and shares them with other teams as appropriate.

KEY MARKERS FOR SUCCESS

Review these key markers for success at the beginning of each year and during the year to keep the professional learning community on track to meet its goals.

- Focus on learning.
- Emphasize what students have learned.
- Students demonstrate proficiency in essential skills.
- Knowledge is shared.
- Common formative assessments are used frequently.
- Assessments identify students who need more support.
- Assessments identify students who can benefit from extended learning opportunities.
- Team members ensure fairness and consistency in assessments.
- Students are supported with systematic and timely responses.
- Flexibility is built into every area of the PLC's operations.
- Collaborative teams in every school share knowledge.
- Practices are shared openly.
- Our focus is on results inside the schools of our district.

NOTES

1. DuFour, Richard. "Common Formative Assessments." *All Things PLC*, July 30, 2017. Retrieved from http://www.allthingsplc.info/blog/view/14/common-formative-assessments.

2. DuFour, Richard, and Mattos, Mike. "How Do Principals Really Improve Schools?" *The Principalship*, vol. 70, no. 7, April 2013. Retrieved from http://www.ascd.org/publications/educational-leadership/apr13/vol70/num07/How-Do-Principals-Really-Improve-Schools¢.aspx.

3. Lewis, Dale, Madison-Harris, Robyn, Mouneke, Ada, and Times, Chris. "Using Data to Guide Instruction and Improve Student Learning." *SEDL Letter*, vol. XXII, no. 2, *Linking Research and Practice*. Retrieved from www.sedl.org/pubs/sedl-letter/v22n02/using-data.html.

4. "Using Assessment in a PLC to Increase Student Learning." Collaborative Teams Network, January 2011. Retrieved from https://wvde.state.wv.us/ctn/Workshop%20Materials/CTN%20January%20Conference/General%20Session%201%20January.pdf.

5. Pandina Scot, Tammy, Callahan, Carolyn, and Urquhart, Jill. "Paint-by-Number Teachers and Cookie-Cutter Students: The Unintended Effects of High-Stakes Testing on the Education of Gifted Students." *Roeper Review*, vol. 31, no. 1: 40–52. December 16, 2008. Retrieved from https://www.tandfonline.com/doi/abs/10.1080/02783190802527364.

6. Schuhl, Sarah. "Using Common Formative and Summative Assessments." Slideshow. Retrieved from http://soltreemrls3.s3-website-us-west-2.amazonaws.com/solution-tree.com/media/pdf/HOE_Schuhl-UsingCommonForm-CFF305.pdf. Accessed September 10, 2018.

7. Wees, David. "Bias in Assessment." *Reflective Educator* (blog), June 11, 2013. Retrieved from https://davidwees.com/content/bias-assessment/.

8. Williams, Teresa Scotton. "Some Issues in the Standardized Testing of Minority Students," *Journal of Education*, vol. 165, no. 2: 192–208, spring 1983. Retrieved from https://www.brighthubeducation.com/student-assessment-tools/65699-standardized-testing-and-cultural-bias/.

5

Digital Expansion

Once your professional learning community has settled into their tasks and duties, take the next step and go digital. Having an online presence will expand your network and allow you to pull in more resources. You'll also be able to share information more easily among schools in your own district and with districts across the nation.

In addition to being online, your PLC will want to adapt digital tools. The variety of apps and software available for educators is broad. You're sure to find at least a few that will become your group's favorites.

This chapter will walk you through a handful of ideas that will get your learning community started. Midrange efforts will expand your network as your group is able to put more effort into their digital footprint. The most technically involved options can be left until later.

THE VALUE OF AN ONLINE PRESENCE

An online presence is a must-have for every organization. Schools and professional learning communities are no exception. These days, being online can supercharge academic growth. The professional learning community can access these benefits only by stepping up their game.

The primary benefit to be garnered from the digital world is connection. When other educators can discover the work your group is doing, they are much more likely to reach out with tips and advice. You'll find, too, that teachers and administrators will more readily seek your advice. You'll help your own students as well as those in other schools.

Being online gives you a gateway into the world. In addition to connecting with American educators, your PLC can keep up with the tips pouring in from other countries. The standards and operations of schools overseas might be different, but the approach to excellence in education is universal.

Many schools have moved from traditional publication methods to online modes.[1] In some cases, parents were the ones who drove the demand. They wanted to be able to access information online, so their districts complied. In other cases, the schools saw that they could reach further into the community through a digital presence.

The same benefits can accrue for your learning community. In addition to broadcasting your group's efforts, accomplishments, and advances, an online presence can be critical in rural areas. Even families that live some distance from their schools can still be actively engaged. Busy suburban and urban parents reap the same benefit when they are able to check in before or after work.

Finally, a digital presence makes communication within your PLC much easier. Ideas that occur to one member can be posted immediately. Conversations can be conducted as individuals have time, which can reduce the need for meeting face-to-face. The recordkeeping aspect is also automatic with most digital tools, which reduces the amount of administrative effort for your group.

INITIAL ONLINE PRESENCE

The first year your PLC comes together, your group has a lot of tasks to accomplish. Getting online might seem like it's not terribly important right away. Having at least a nominal digital presence, however, will empower your group to reap benefits right away.

Starting small will open the door. Find out what kinds of online venues are already being maintained by your school or district. Most schools will already have a website. These websites often include portals visitors enter to gather information or to send communications to the staff.

An example might be a school that hosts one or more blogs on their website. One blog might be "outward facing," or accessible to the public, so that parents can learn about special events. A different blog might be "inward facing" and accessible only to users who log in through the school's system.

Both kinds of blogs can be great places for the PLCs to announce their presence, share new documents, and post short articles or information about milestones. Blogs that are inward facing offer you a peer-to-peer communication channel. Outward-facing blogs provide transparency for your learning group.

Your next step should be to consider social networking sites. These networks, like Twitter, Facebook, and LinkedIn, allow users to create individual profiles. All of them have the option to create profiles for organizations, so it's likely that your schools or your district have at least one active account already.

Check with each school to see how often your PLC can provide short updates on those profile feeds. The updates should be short enough to fit with what users are looking for. That's great because short posts are often easy to generate. Have the same information reposted several times to ensure that everyone gets a chance to see it.

Social media does, however, have the drawback of expecting multiple posts. If you're managing one or more feeds yourself, spread out the burden. Task each planning group with creating one post on a rotating basis. If you have four planning groups, each group will provide one social media post each month. This covers all four weeks of an average month.

To help keep things on track, pick a single due date for all four groups. Provide all four posts to the school's media coordinator, and have them send out one post each week. If the coordinator can schedule a regular day and time, interested users can look for the updates from your learning group on the same day each week.

EXPANDING YOUR ONLINE PRESENCE

As noted in the previous section, using the school's existing online elements will help your team stay focused on startup activities while keeping the larger community updated. Once you're ready for the next step, consider some of the ideas in this section to boost the power of your online efforts.

First, set up at least one social media service for the professional learning group. You might find that using the same platform as the school will help you attract followers more quickly. However, you'll also be competing for attention with the school with every post on that platform.

Instead, consider using a different social media site for your group. This will help you connect with individuals who might not have signed up for the school's feed because they only use that site for personal posts. Generate a crosscurrent of member signups by sharing the school's updates on your social media page. Both will benefit by keeping more parents, educators, and community members informed.

Second, set up a blog on a free hosting site. If the school or district already maintains a blog on their website, ask them to create another for your group. When the PLC has their own blog, they can post updates as quickly as needed. Your members will also be able to call for assistance from specific groups like educators or parents.

And, of course, you'll have complete control over the blog. Your learning community will be in charge of how often to post and the content of each post. Whenever you locate a new resource, visitors can write guest entries. With this type of control, you will be in complete charge of the messages.

Work sharing can easily be set up for this format. Each team should be responsible for a set number of blog posts in their area every month. Train one person on each team in making the posts and other administrative work relating to blog maintenance. Also task each planning group with locating one guest blogger per quarter.

Once the group is comfortable with the social media and blog schedule, select a visual social media account. Try Flickr, YouTube, or Vimeo. All three will allow you to share short videos. The posts will be an invaluable way to add a lot of impact to your outreach and communication.

Best of all, most smartphones and laptops let you shoot video easily. Whenever one person from your team attends a conference or workshop, have them take a series of pictures for the blog or a quick two-minute video for the video site. When they return, post the pictures or video along with brief comments about the experience.

To extend the useful life of your images and videos, consider writing a blog entry about them at some future point. Add links from the blog to the video, and from the video to the blog. Then followers in each place can find new content on your other social media profiles.

Be sure to maximize the use of your content by recycling. Repost links to pictures and videos the following year. As a conference or workshop draws near, post last year's content with new comments about what you're looking forward to in the upcoming experience.

Remember that the images don't have to be professionally produced. The quality achieved by most smartphones and tablets is good enough. Your goal is to provide moments from the event, not to document the proceedings in detail.

Once you've started down this path, try to post one video every month and one photo every week. Each team can take up the task on a rotating basis. You can even provide pictures or short videos of moments when the PLC interacts with educators. Show warm greetings, teamwork in action, or a brief, informative clip from a conversation.

Pictures and videos allow individuals who might never meet you in person to really connect with the PLC. When they see that real people are providing genuine assistance to their schools, they will be much more likely to volunteer. The ties between your learning community and other PLCs will also grow stronger.

DOCUMENTS AND FILES

Technology provides excellent ways for professional learning groups to upgrade their operations. In addition to the sharing opportunities afforded by the internet, a variety of apps and software can change the way a group collaborates. You can even take collective action with digital tools.

The success of every PLC revolves around these three aspects, so the decision to use digital tools will help you achieve your goals. Your learning community can develop content with the input of other groups and share ideas as they arise. You can even form subcommittees in new communities and meet virtually.

To share documents, try Google Drive or Dropbox. They both offer free-service levels, and the free levels come with plenty of storage. The advantage of either of these services is that individuals and groups can easily share large files.

When you want to disseminate information to a large number of people, try services like PBWorks. The pages you create with these tools are like websites that every user can add to and edit. PBWorks offers free membership for educators. Wikispaces has taken specific steps to meet the needs of educators.

To boost your ability to share materials in a more interactive way, consider a social bookmarking service like Diigo. Users of these services can work as a team to develop a collection of useful websites. Categorize the sites by topic or curricular area to build an expansive and dynamic resource.

One of the best parts of a bookmarking service is the annotation feature. Anyone can highlight portions of articles they post, ask questions related to the text, and see the answers added by others. Diigo provides free accounts for educators. Those accounts can be accessed by multiple individuals.

COLLECTIVE EFFORTS

In any professional learning group, working toward the same goal is a given. The members originally came together to enhance academic achievement. The goals your group set focus on educational success. In nearly every case, you'll reach those goals faster with digital tools that allow for collective efforts.

Collective work can be performed online at any time and from any location with internet access. The convenience alone allows for a much greater degree of flexibility and inclusion. Your PLC will capture more input and effort when individuals can log on when it's convenient.

First, look for tools that allow group members to work together even when they can't meet face to face. Live chat tools like Chatzy provide private channels for conversations. Skype can handle multiple lines for fully digital meetings. They can also allow individuals who can't attend a meeting in person to join in.

Apps for interactive whiteboards, electronic polls, voice recorders linked to documents or videos, and many others are available. Once you start looking, you'll find a lot of options that will fit your PLC's needs.

Next, your learning community should investigate task-specific tools. Some sites, like MasteryConnect, are designed to handle specific educational areas like assessment data. To make collection easier, MasteryConnect, Socrative, and Plickers use cameras to record data. Plickers can even handle situations where only one individual has access to a digital device.

A list of common tools is found at the end of this chapter. When you begin the search, don't look at what's available. The sheer number of tools will be overwhelming. Instead, consider which specific task needs to be accomplished. Focus in on the task and look for tools that solve only that task. Your search will be much more productive.

Once you've set up your digital toolbox, consider when to allow others access to your task-specific tools. When your group is first formed, your PLC will focus on finding the people who can best help on a day-to-day basis. At some point, you'll want to pull in people who aren't in your district or even in your state.

Casting the net wide is going to be much easier using digital tools. Consider opening up certain segments of your collaborative workspaces to PLCs in other schools or districts. Be sure to protect areas that you want to remain accessible only to the group. Then your discussions will remain private until you're ready to release information.

ADAPT DIGITAL TOOLS

When your group has narrowed its list of digital tools to only a few, consider both the current moment and the learning community's future. Even though everyone in the group today might be comfortable with a specific technology, membership will change every year. Tools that are too technical might be a source of issues for new people.

Before settling on a specific tool, ask whether it can be integrated seamlessly. The greatest challenge of educational technology is not necessarily the cost of the tool or the time needed to locate the best tool. Instead, the support offered to the individuals who must use those tools commonly presents issues.[2]

The effectiveness of any tool depends on the skill of its user. When looking at apps and software, pick ones with intuitive dashboards. Go a step further and provide documents, written in plain language, that explain how to implement the tool. Always offer to send someone in person to help with setup and to troubleshoot issues.

During your PLC's initial years and anytime a reorganization occurs, build a ladder that allows for easy integration. Implement one foundational tool or software. Give the group plenty of time to grow comfortable with that tool before introducing another. Learning together will also enhance the connections among the community's members.

Also consider using the same approach for introducing new members to the learning community. Give them the same tools in the same order. Ease them into using the tools at their own pace. Because the entire group will be available to help, their learning curve will be much easier to climb.

This on-the-ground approach is particularly useful because it allows for adjustments based on real experiences. As the PLC becomes more familiar with the foundational tool set, they might discover that some of the other tools they had planned to integrate later aren't going to work.

When one tool is added at a time, the learning community avoids time-consuming problems with integration. Your group will be much less likely to end up stuck with something that doesn't work well. You'll feel empowered to make changes that really matter as soon as the issues begin to appear.

DIGITAL TOOLS FOR THE CLASSROOM

In addition to the tools your professional learning group uses for its own work, you can offer teachers apps and software designed for classroom use. This can be as easy as collecting a list of useful tools or as complex as distributing a specific app to every educator.

When a PLC takes on this kind of effort, they ease the burden on educators. New teachers who have little experience might be overwhelmed by the sheer number of tools at their disposal. Research and recommendations made by the PLC and the PLC's network can reduce the amount of time they spend searching for the right item.

Teachers who are implementing new initiatives in their classrooms can benefit the same way. Using the shared resources provided by the learning group, they can more easily locate exactly what they need. The fact that those recommendations often come from other educators also provides a built-in pathway for help. They can be confident that any issues integrating or using the tool will be answered by someone who understands their situation.

The greatest benefits derived from digital tools increase over time. Educators who can see how well fellow teachers fare with specific tools are more likely to adapt those tools. When enough teachers use the same apps or software, their ability to share, collaborate, and work collectively grows. They might not become their own PLC, but they certainly will act like one.

INSTANT UPDATES AND MOTIVATION

The PLC can use tools in a variety of ways. In addition to data gathering and formal elements, the group's motivation and communication can benefit.

AnswerGarden, for example, is an online tool that generates word clouds based on user responses to prompts. Your PLC leader might ask how the team feels about the progress made toward a certain goal. In response, each group member offers a single word that captures what they think.

This tool can be a great way to judge how things are going between meetings. It can also be a wonderful motivational tool that keeps everyone focused. Offering this to classroom educators can be beneficial when students generate word clouds related to class assignments or projects.

Its most powerful use comes when it is offered to the public. Parents can be asked to send in a single word in response to prompts about student performance, school facilities, or a project the team is considering. Generating a word cloud that is shared through social media can help the public see the very real benefits associated with your group's efforts.

Other word-cloud generators include Tagul, ABCya, and TagCrowd.

TIPS FOR SHARING

- On social media, follow users with similar interests to those of your group.
- Locate and follow hashtags related to the PLC's goals and interests.
- Don't be shy about sharing content. Sharing adds value for your followers and attracts new followers.
- Followers are a great resource. Tap them whenever you have issues that need new, out-of-the-box solutions.
- Rather than trying to read every message that comes through on active social media tools, scan the posts for a few minutes to see what pops out.
- Links can be shortened for posting using Bitly or TinyURL.
- Every link should include a note about what the link will yield.
- Link to the PLC's blog whenever a social media post is relevant to something the group has written about in depth.
- Posts that include images always generate a stronger response than posts without an image.
- Always link to all social media on which the learning community appears.

TIPS FOR COLLABORATION

- No matter how your group decides to share materials, create a common naming structure for uploaded files.
- Agree on different types of categories and subcategories for different types of materials. This will keep your group's resources organized.
- All materials should have a brief written description of the content posted with the materials.
- Materials that can be associated with more than one category should be posted to the category where they have the most impact. Post only the brief description in the other categories. Include a link to the material.
- Set up templates for documents that are frequently used to ensure consistency.
- Conclusions that arise from conversations among specific groups, like planning teams, can be written and posted. These updates can be used as resources for groups facing similar issues.
- Recognize that the resources you share don't have to be groundbreaking. They do, however, have to be useful, effective, and efficient.
- Remember that with more sharing comes greater opportunities to collaborate.

TIPS FOR COLLECTIVE DIGITAL EFFORTS

- When looking for digital tools, consider the task to be conducted first.
- Whenever your group identifies a digital tool that yields strong results, incorporate it into the standard procedures.

- Ensure that every individual associated with the PLC is offered assistance that respects their current level of achievement.
- Reduce effort with digital tools that meet specific needs.
- Select apps and software that are intuitive and that don't need a lot of training to use.
- Ensure that every individual associated with the PLC, including educators and administrators who are not part of the group, are updated regularly about the group's selections.
- Respect the choice of individual educators to use digital tools they have selected themselves.

ASSESSING DIGITAL TOOLS

Before adopting a digital tool, have every member fill out this questionnaire. The group can then discuss potential issues and determine whether the tool is really the right fit.

How will this tool be used by the group?
_____
_____

Is this tool easy to begin using? Is the dashboard intuitive? Are the instructions clear and concise?
_____
_____

How easily can this tool be integrated with existing tools/procedures? If this is a foundational tool, how easily can other tools be integrated with it in the future?
_____
_____

If the group decides to exchange this tool for a different one later on, how easily can the data stored in this tool be transferred to other tools?
_____
_____

Will this technology provide immediate results? If not, will the value of the results be equal to or greater than the investment of time and effort?
_____
_____
_____

Can this single tool be utilized in different ways to achieve different goals?

What benefits do you foresee in adopting this specific tool?

What issues do you think might arise if this tool is adopted?

What solutions might answer potential issues that arise from using this tool?

Is the tool primarily to be used to achieve depth of results or results that are broad?

Can a modular approach (using more than one digital tool) achieve the same results with greater efficiency or more effectively?

Is the tool provided by a company that can provide support over the long term?

COMMON CLASSROOM DIGITAL TOOLS

When assessing digital tools for your professional learning community, consider tools that many classrooms are already using. Utilize the same or similar tools whenever possible to allow your group to connect, collaborate, and work collectively with educators right from the start. Here's a list of the common types of tools seen in classrooms today.

- Annotation tools
- Journaling apps and/or classroom blogs
- Avatars, simple icons, or digitally created animations, that represent an individual

- File-sharing tools
- Back-channel tools, which allow multiple users to listen in on one-way communication
- Calendar tools
- Online quizzes, polls, and games
- Class website and social media pages
- Digital portfolios
- Email groups
- Flipped classroom tools that create learner-centered instruction
- Virtual meeting tools
- Video sharing sites

TOP DIGITAL TOOLS FOR PLCs

Considering every tool your professional learning community could use would be overwhelming. Instead, use this list to help you focus on the most useful ones. Then, over time, your group can add additional apps that fit specific needs.

- An RSS feed to aggregate new content without having to perform searches
- An RSS reader to make reading RSS feed results easier
- An annotation service
- A social bookmarking service so you can share bookmarked web pages
- A digital bulletin board
- A digital notebook
- Social networking pages
- A dedicated blog
- An online meeting site
- A flowchart-, diagram-, and graph-creation tool
- Photo sharing site
- Video sharing site
- A slideshow or presentation app
- A calendar or scheduling tool
- Email or other group-communication method

NOTES

1. "How Important for Schools to Have an Online Presence." *Schoolchalao*. Medium, October 10, 2017. Retrieved from https://medium.com/@schoolchalaoalwar/how-important-for-schools-to-have-an-online-presence-13e0912e6de1.

2. "21st Century Learning Environments." Partnership for 21st Century Skills, August 22, 2018. Retrieved from http://www.p21.org/storage/documents/le_white_paper-1.pdf.

6

Sail on Course

Educators and educational administrators face a number of challenges. Overcrowded classrooms, the effort involved with testing and assessment, and limited resources all take attention away from teaching. Fortunately, the professional learning group can help alleviate pressure in many of these areas.

But what about the members of your group? They have to deal with the PLC's challenges. Even simple issues, when they pile up, can make staying focused difficult. This is especially true because the learning community has a mission. A challenge that presents itself when the group is fully engaged in the mission's goals can seem overwhelming.

Awareness is one of your best tools. Forewarned, as they say, is forearmed. By being aware of the kinds of problems that might arise, your group can have ideas and operations in place to tackle each type. In this chapter, we'll consider the top issues facing professional learning communities nationwide.

INFORMATION INDIGESTION

In "5 Common Mistakes When Starting a PLC (and How to Avoid Them)," a focus that is too broad makes the list.[1] Avoid this issue by being aware of it during the goal-setting stage. Your group should specify the grade level or population being targeted, describe learner goals, and define specific desired outcomes.

The same is true when the learning community starts any research. A number of the digital tools discussed in the previous chapter allow members to easily collect links. If the links are not chosen wisely, however, the resource can choke the group with too much information.

Enthusiasm at the beginning of any stage can make members feel as if they will go to any lengths. With that mindset, more resources are better than fewer resources. To keep things manageable, set boundaries for every topic.

Limit the information to be shared to studies and papers generated by well-respected national education groups. Narrow the search to specific grade levels, curricular topics, or teaching methods. Drill down to the details of the task to be accomplished. Put aside the broad studies in favor of ones that target your group, your students, and your needs.

These boundaries should be set by the planning groups. Each planning team should break their primary goal down into smaller units, where information is required. Since academic skills like reading comprehension and mathematics are different at different grades, the research should narrowly target the grade level in question.

The research results will end up being much more relevant. The materials the planning team has to review in order to formulate their activities will be better focused. Efficiency produces better results when the team zooms in on the target and conserves the efforts needed to achieve the goal.

WILTING ENTHUSIASM

The academic year can seem like a slough even as the days fly past. Professional learning communities with the best of intentions can find that their group isn't as motivated as it was in earlier days. This can happen in the middle of the year or, if your membership stays the same from year to year, later in the journey.

One solution is found in something your group is likely doing all the time anyway: recruitment. By pulling in new individuals as members or as temporary experts, the atmosphere of collegial effort is refreshed. Parents who participate also enliven the group.

Remember that students can revitalize your PLC. Be sure that the group is reaching out regularly to student councils, extracurricular clubs, and specific populations. Surveys are a great way to garner new ideas. You might sponsor special events or activities that foster academic achievement throughout the year.

Another way to keep the energy high is to rotate duties. Try not to burden the same individual with the same types of administrative or officer duties every year. Research and outreach components should be assigned to different individuals every month. With this last point, you'll ensure that the PLC's perspective remains inclusive and diverse.

Your physical surroundings can also be manipulated. Consider meeting in different venues every month. Gather in a café near the school so that everyone can sip a cup of tea. Schedule breaks during the meetings that are long enough to allow individuals to chat.

Don't overlook new ways to build relationships. Host a quarterly potluck that is geared to socializing rather than tasks. Individuals who know each other feel more comfortable working together. They can recognize the stressors that affect others and offer help.

The more you mix it up, the better off your group will be. They'll know that they are part of a community because relationships within that community are constantly revitalized. The PLC will stay on track to meet its goals while forming a tightknit group of like-minded educators.

DYSFUNCTIONAL ROLES

Your learning group will be made up of individuals who come from a variety of backgrounds. Their life experiences, and their experiences as educators, will vary as much as their backgrounds. Because of factors like these, members will not agree on every item.

Disagreements are healthy. They open the door to conversations that can uncover potential flaws. The group's wealth of knowledge allows the PLC to make corrections before a good idea turns bad. And, of course, disagreements can lead to new ideas that are far superior to the original.

In some instances, though, individual members will not be able to agree fully. Most of the time, this will not hamper achievement. Someone might not care for a particular teaching method being proposed, but will willingly champion it because the technique works for most educators.

What about those times when the entire group cannot reach a consensus? Steven Weber wrote about just such problems in "Five Dysfunctions of a Professional Learning Community."[2] After years of watching educators struggle with teamwork and shared resources, he pinpointed several areas where dysfunctional dynamics threaten to upend PLC efforts.

Three out of those five came down to how individuals work together or fail to work together. All three of those are related to communication. When every member of the learning group recognizes that the PLC has specific operational procedures, they are able to understand why those procedures are in place. Respect for those decisions generates healthy interactions.

At the start of every academic year, and when new members are introduced during the academic year, review the reasoning behind these decisions. This review informs new members about the expectations surrounding their approach to other team members. It also reminds existing members of the attitude they should demonstrate.

Another key element is to ensure that communication channels are easy to use, inclusive, and free-flowing. Every PLC should specify which e-mails, discussion threads, or social media posts are required and which are optional. The ones related to PLC issues, goals, and activities must be utilized by every member.

Occasionally, a learning group discovers that trust has been broken. Somewhere along the line, one or more individuals felt they could no longer count on other members. It might have been caused by a casual comment shared outside the meeting, or it could have been caused by a more dramatic rupture.

A lack of trust can point to deeper challenges. When the group cannot count on others to be honest and open, problems are bound to occur. A teacher who cannot admit weakness isn't going to work exceptionally hard to face challenges.

In these cases, an intervention might be required. The leader of the PLC or the individual's planning team should start with a private conversation. Note the issue, and ask the individual to discuss the reasons for taking a particular tactic.

Often the leader will discover that the lack of trust springs from an area that can be resolved with a little guidance. Perhaps this person tried a similar approach in the past only to fail. They have lost faith in their group's direction because of their past experience.

Encourage an open debate. Begin the discussion of the issue during the private conversation. Then, once the leader and the member grasp the nuances, bring the discussion to the group. Honest and open explorations lead to solutions everyone can agree on.

WHY PLCs FAIL

EducationWorld listed five common reasons why professional learning communities fail to meet their goals.[3] The issues they listed can be grouped into two areas. First among these is the culture surrounding the learning community. Second is the availability of resources and how those resources are used.

The culture of your group is one of the most important keys to immediate and sustainable success. Everyone who comes on board, whether they join at the beginning or arrive years later, should understand the demands. Clearly lay out the kinds of duties individuals take on. Help each member determine whether they can handle the commitment.

Garnering group consensus is also key to a functional culture. Whenever your PLC sets a new goal, the decision to undertake that task should be based on input and recommendations from the educational community. Share information about how other schools and other learning communities have approached the issue.

Be selective about what your group tackles. Ensure that every goal can be achieved with current resources or resources that can be gathered. Determine which goals will truly impact academic achievement. Target specific areas in terms of curriculum, grade level, and desired outcome.

Maintain an attitude that communicates your group's enthusiasm and their genuine desire to help. Ensure that your learning community is accessible to everyone involved with your schools and district. Keep the channels open so that new ideas flow in. Regularly update your community through social media and other pathways.

All these steps will ensure that the culture of your professional learning community is built for productivity. Individuals who contribute to your projects will feed off that passion. A motivated team creates and strengthens a culture that is open and enthusiastic.

Even better, the strong culture will help you address issues related to resources. This direct relationship occurs because an open culture fosters a larger network. With a broad reach, your learning community can access individuals who can locate new resources, new funding sources, and new experts.

Don't be shy in asking for help. PLCs have a much greater pull with the community than individual educators do. The fact that your group is an organization gives you more credentials. When you reach out to businesses or nonprofits, your requests will much more likely be taken seriously.

When considering the best use of resources, prioritize your group's goals. Funnel the largest amount of resources toward the top goal. Disperse the rest according to the importance of the other tasks. As each goal is met, release remaining resources along the same pattern, with the greater number of resources allocated to the most important.

Embed tasks into the workday whenever possible. Your updates might go out as part of the school's regular newsletter. Co-teaching sessions can allow an experienced teacher to train another educator in the PLC's recommended methods. When the duties are embedded into usual workday activities, progress is made quickly. Success becomes more likely.

Monitor how resources are utilized as the learning community moves forward. This allows your group to shift underutilized elements to areas that need more support. Your learning community will also discover how to utilize resources in ways that ensure success.

Coordinating the use of resources can enhance their effectiveness. One individual might be needed during the first stage of one effort, but their involvement becomes less critical as the project moves forward. If they can be moved to a different area and utilized more effectively there, do so.

Resources of time, money, effort, and experiences are precious in every district. By administering them with these several key elements in mind, your PLC will be able to do more with what's already available.

AVOID A MAJOR CRISIS

In a study conducted by Cornerstone at the Minnesota State University, Mankato,[4] one difficult issue for professional learning communities involved individuals outside the PLC. School boards, superintendents, and state and federal organizations are often not easily influenced by individual schools.

External stakeholders like these can create difficulties large enough to upend your group's efforts. Your learning community should keep this in mind whenever you start a new initiative. Communication with the external groups and individuals will go a long way toward eliminating potential problems.

The mission of your group is to enhance education. The same priority is clearly part of the mandates of these external stakeholders. Remain focused on that single common goal every time your group interacts with outsiders. This reminds everyone that you are working together for the same achievement: excellence in learning.

Clarity and specificity will always generate the best results. Provide information that has been boiled down to the primary points. Offer brief details about milestones and expected results. Then, if more information is required, more details can be provided.

Make sure that the PLC's goals align with the summative assessments and standardized testing required by state and federal governments. Your group's goal should be connected to these elements from the beginning. Alignment allows for easier implementation in the classroom.

Make sure that others can clearly see the alignment. It might seem obvious to your learning community, but it might not be so obvious to others. Demonstrate exactly how your group's efforts support mandates, and your learning community will be much more likely to receive support.

When necessary, reach out to influencers who can help smooth communications. Superintendents who resist your group's efforts might listen to principals who praise the benefits their students receive. School boards will be motivated to support your learning community's vision when they hear that the superintendent has provided critical resources.

This shared vision is the engine that propels your group forward. The external stakeholders need to recognize, at every step, that your purpose and your intentions are geared toward academic excellence. The results that you share will confirm that their faith in your PLC was well founded.

CLIMATE CONTROL

The other major barrier Cornerstone discussed was a school's climate. The environment in which your learning community works has a huge impact on the success or failure of your projects. When educators don't accept the learning community's recommendations, milestones are missed. Targeted activities go off course.

Principals can be your best resource. They can work with teachers to discover why the resistance arose. Time is of course a major factor. Educators who already feel overburdened might feel burdened by more work. This could be especially true if the PLC is proposing something without proof that it will succeed.

Once the issues come to light, they can be addressed. Principals or individuals from the PLC can work to reduce educators' overall workload. Often this means showing them ways to be more productive. In other cases, the process might reveal that individuals have taken on tasks that don't belong to them.

Either way, an attitude of open inquiry and a real willingness to help go a long way. Because resolving issues often produces more efficient procedures, the teacher in question is the biggest winner. And that means they become the learning community's biggest fan.

Although principals are key in many areas of the school climate, other factors play a role. In small schools, there might be only a single educator who teaches a particular topic. How is that person supposed to develop common assessments if they are the only one working in that area?

The answer lies in the larger community, and in the network of individuals discovered through outreach efforts. Link the single teacher with individuals from other schools or districts who work in the same area. In addition to being able to perform the task, they'll benefit from having new individuals to call on.

Another answer lies in cross-curricular elements. Reading comprehension or mathematical ability, both broad areas, can be targeted in a number of curricular areas. For goals that focus on more specialized skills, expand the search to the district or across the state. Connecting individuals to others who teach in the same area or in cross-curricular areas allows them to work with a team toward a common target.

A controlled climate produces an environment in which your PLC's efforts can soar.

BEST RESEARCH PRACTICES

- Define a specific question to drive the research.
- Identify possible sources of information.
- Judge the scope of research required. If necessary, redefine the question to make it more specific.
- Assign the appropriate number of team members to the research.
- Schedule a time frame in which the research is to be completed.
- Explore a variety of resources such as texts, internet searches, videos and podcasts, and seminars or workshops.
- Each member should write a synopsis of the results informed by their research.
- Discuss the results with the entire PLC/planning team.
- Schedule a time frame in which additional research can be performed (if required).
- Schedule a time frame during which all team members can review targeted sources (if required).
- Reconvene with the purpose of sharing new information.
- Generate a decision.

RECHARGE THE PLC

- Consider whether procedures followed during the meetings are truly the most efficient and effective.
- Relieve pressure on specific team members by breaking their duties down into components that can be handed off to others.

- Reach out to your network for tips and advice on how they refresh commitment and motivation.
- Every academic year, offer the group one or more opportunities to gather socially.
- Start each meeting by observing five minutes of silence. Encourage members to sit quietly rather than using the time to catch up on work.
- Every month, schedule time during a meeting to watch a short TED Talk on education, academic achievement, or learning.
- Assign the PLC members movies or novels set in schools as a fun way to spur conversations and new ideas.
- Review accomplishments the PLC reached during the previous year, the previous term, or the previous week. Focus on what's working well.
- Give credit where credit is due. Publically praise individuals, planning teams, and the schools when they reach targeted goals.

TEAM TRUST SURVEY

Answer the following questions by ranking responses from 1 (agree) to 3 (disagree).

_____My team members share their materials, resources, and ideas with the PLC.
_____I feel comfortable sharing my materials, resources, and ideas with the PLC.
_____I am welcomed by my PLC/planning team at every meeting.
_____I believe that my team members have good intentions.
_____I believe that my team members are competent and capable educators.
_____I can count on my fellow team members.
_____My team members help me grow as an educational professional.
_____Everyone on my team is working toward the same goal.
_____Everyone on my team makes significant contributions that help reach the PLC's goals.
_____My entire team celebrates individual and collective accomplishments.
_____My team members critique efforts in ways that are constructive and helpful.
_____My PLC has a positive reputation in the educational community it serves.
_____My PLC is making a positive impact in the educational community.

EXERCISES FOR BUILDING TRUST

Offer a **storytelling hour** during which educators can relay stories about their work. Each hour should revolve around a theme such as "the power of teaching" or "why educators choose to be educators."

Set up a **display case** in each school. Ask the staff to donate an item that represents a significant moment in their careers. Pair each item with a phrase or a brief note about what the item represents. As the case fills, group the items into whichever categories naturally arise.

Set up a locked **disaster day** box in the meeting room. Anyone can anonymously drop in a letter about a real disaster they experienced as an educator or sound off about their frustrations. Every month, gather the group together and run all the responses, unread, through a shredder. Encourage everyone to release the disaster and the frustration, and move forward to a better outcome.

At the beginning of every meeting, **share praise.** Working around the table, have the team offer one positive thing they noted about each member. Limit the responses to a single good thing. This way, everyone feels equally appreciated.

Hang a **photo board** in the meeting room or set one up on Pinterest. Allow members to post pictures of classrooms and students who have benefited from the PLC's efforts. Add captions to each picture, and let the public see the students and your group in action.

COURSE ADJUSTMENTS

As milestones are achieved, consider the following questions to determine whether adjustments need to be made by the planning teams.

How can teachers' instructional schedules be adjusted to allow enough common time for collaboration?
_____
_____

Should certain staff members be released from other duties so that their full attention can be dedicated to a specific goal? If so, which duties should be removed?
_____
_____

Are additional or different funds, materials, or other resources required to meet the goal? If so, what are those resources, and in what quantity are they needed?
_____
_____

Is the implementation of the goal aligned with state and federal mandates? If not, how have efforts deviated during implementation?
_____
_____

Do the leaders of each teacher team require more support in order to be effective? If so, what type of support do they require?

_____
_____
_____

Is the culture surrounding the PLC positive and effective? If not, how could it be changed?

_____
_____
_____

Is the climate within the school positive and supportive of the PLC? If not, how might this be changed?

_____
_____
_____

DISTRICT-WIDE IMPACT

The most effective professional learning community enables the entire district to come together for a common goal. Academic achievement is at the top of every school's priority list, so form a PLC that generates district-wide results. After your group has settled in, consider the following steps to optimize results across the district.

- Each school should share a commitment to superior educational results for all students.
- Teachers in different schools should be given time to organize teams that can collaborate for a singular goal.
- The planning teams should share their materials with planning teams that hold similar goals.
- Assessments and other materials should be adapted for cross-curricular use whenever possible.
- Each school must create and maintain a system of intervention to support students who are having difficulty.
- Each school must create and maintain a plan for extending the enrichment of high-performing students at every grade level and in every curricular area.
- Administrative staff should emphasize collaborative efforts that promote the PLC's progress.
- Leaders at every level should take an interest in and support the PLC's goals.

NOTES

1. "5 Common Mistakes When Starting a PLC (and How to Avoid Them)." *WeAreTeachers*, June 21, 2012. Retrieved from https://www.weareteachers.com/5-common-mistakes-when-starting-a-plc-and-how-to-avoid-them-2/.

2. Weber, Steven. "Five Dysfunctions of a Professional Learning Community." *The Whole Child*, October 26, 2011. Retrieved from http://www.wholechildeducation.org/blog/five-dysfunctions-of-a-professional-learning-community.

3. Provini, Celine. "Why Don't Professional Learning Communities Work?" *Education World*, 2013. Retrieved from https://www.educationworld.com/a_admin/professional-learning-community-pitfalls-best-practices.shtml.

4. Clarke, Katie Carol. "The Identification of Successes and Barriers in Establishing Professional Learning Communities from Principals' Perspectives." University of Minnesota at Mankato, 2014. Retrieved from https://cornerstone.lib.mnsu.edu/cgi/viewcontent.cgi?referer=https://www.bing.com/&httpsredir=1&article=1340&context=etds.

Appendix

Stepping onto the PLC Highway

Congratulations! Your professional learning community has put in the teamwork, trust, and collaborative effort needed to launch a new phase for your schools and your district. Your dedication to reflective practices will enhance the abilities of every educational professional your group encounters.

The real winners in this are the students and your community. The gains in academic achievement demonstrated by the students will bring pride to parents and administrators. When these young people graduate and enter the world, they will make lasting contributions to your community and the world.

As your learning community advanced through the six chapters of this book, your group considered the six key steps to creating and maintaining a successful PLC. New members will want to read through this entire book, from start to finish. At any point, other members can do the same.

Your group can also turn to this final section for a quick review. The following pages are short refreshers that remind you of the key components of each chapter. Each refresher condenses the core components of the six steps into a brief set of points.

These refreshers can be your guides for setting annual goals, implementing quarterly reviews, and closing out the previous year. They are also invaluable reminders of the compass points on your map. With a quick read-through of these pages, you will recall your PLC's exact focus, attitude, and best practices.

REFRESHER 1:
LAY THE FOUNDATION

Building Blocks

- Reflective practices lead to true learning.
- Focus on learning over teaching.
- Dialog among educators shares ideas, supports diversity, and generates ingenuity.
- Shared responsibility enhances collaboration.
- Shared values generate cohesive focus and action.
- Shared norms create the PLC's culture.
- Common practices clear the way for academic achievement.
- Feedback enables change.

Create the PLC

- Collaboration and trust allow for true teamwork and inclusivity.
- Inclusiveness and shared responsibility strengthen PLC projects.
- Focus on solutions to create real and lasting change.
- Steps to take:
    - Set a schedule.
    - Select a facilitator.
    - Define the environment.
- Enhance knowledge.

Revitalize an Existing PLC

- Integrate new members with information.
- Reach out to gather ideas and feedback from nonmembers.
- Celebrate milestones and praise achievements.

REFRESHER 2:
GATHER THE GOALS

- Generate broad goals.
- Pinpoint the differences between schools, populations, grades, etc.
- Set initial goals for specific schools, populations, grade levels, etc.
- Set specific goals targeting the challenges facing each subgroup.
- Determine how to nurture positive growth.
- Pinpoint potential obstacles.

- Locate unique elements associated with specific subgroups, the PLC, or the community.
- Assist educators with setting individual goals.
- Prioritize the goals.
- Group similar goals.
- Pair resources and educational professionals with each group of goals.

REFRESHER 3: GOING LIVE

- Return to the original focus on learning as a touchstone.
- Determine the essential outcomes for the current year.
- Consider connection points that will streamline effort.
- Assign planning teams to the goals.
- Each team determines the resources required to reach their goals.
- Consider which evidence-based instructional strategy to use.
- Develop a common lesson plan that will meet the goals and outcomes.
- Encourage the use and sharing of teaching portfolios.
- Ask the entire community to help implement common lesson plans.
- Personalize the implementation for each classroom.

REFRESHER 4: ASSESS AND ADAPT

- Determine which assessments will provide the most powerful results.
- Eliminate existing assessments that don't function well for your school or district.
- Wrap existing assessments into more powerful assessments or replace as appropriate.
- Determine how often to implement assessments.
- Schedule the assessments.
- Assessment targets:
    - Student learning.
    - Students with additional needs (those facing difficulties).
    - Learners who can broaden their scope of learning (high performers).
- Analyze data to determine whether the goals are realistic and challenging.
- Encourage group goal setting to enhance outcomes.
- Assessment foundation should be:

- Data driven.
- Measurable.
- Efficient.
- Assessments should include:
  - Student demographics.
  - Learning skills relative to mandates/standards.
  - Disciplinary statistics.
- Value formative over summative assessments.
- Avoid assessment bias.

REFRESHER 5: DIGITAL EXPANSION

- Utilize existing school/district online spaces for announcements.
  - School or district website/s.
  - School or district public blog/s.
  - School or district internal blog/s.
  - Social networking sites.
- Create/refresh the PLC's online presence.
  - Website accessible to the public (teachers, parents, schools, the district, etc.).
  - Chat tools and material-sharing sites for member use.
  - Public blog.
  - Social media profiles.
- Set up/refresh media sharing.
  - Flickr or other photo-sharing account.
  - YouTube, Vimeo, or other video-sharing account.
- Select/review current apps and software.
  - Document sharing and file sharing.
  - Mini-website or Wiki-style entries for sharing information with nonmembers.
  - Social bookmarking and annotation service.
- Select/review existing tools for collective effort.
  - Assessment data tools.
  - Live chat tools.
  - Interactive whiteboards.
  - Electronic polls.
  - Voice recorders.
- Plan for seamless integration of all digital tools and software.
- Maintain a database of how-to instructions for each tool.
- Curate a list of digital tools recommended for classroom use.

REFRESHER 6:
SAIL ON COURSE

- Awareness of potential issues is the best defense against problems.
- Keep goals specific and tightly focused.
- Manage resources with careful curation.
- Set boundaries on research efforts.
- Recruit new members to keep enthusiasm high.
- Remain open to fresh perspectives.
- Rotate duties among members.
- Provide social opportunities for the group.
- Recognize the opportunities embedded in disagreements.
- Respectfully agree to disagree.
- Clearly communicate expectations for PLC members.
- Maintain open channels of communication.
- Nurture trust.
- Cultivate a culture that is open, enthusiastic, and motivated.
- Prioritize goals and assign resources appropriately.
- Monitor how resources are utilized, and reassign resources as opportunities arise.
- Inform external stakeholders (the school board, superintendent, and other organizations).
- Align the PLC's goals with state and federal requirements.
- Reach out to influencers who can help.
- Cultivate a climate of open inquiry and support.

About the Author

Barbara D. Culp has devoted the past forty-four years to education. After teaching at the elementary and middle-school levels for fifteen years, she was promoted to a principalship. Shortly before retiring, she was selected as Principal of the Year. She went on to work for eight years as a part-time clinical supervisor for Brenau University's School of Education. During that time, she began pursuing one of her passions, helping struggling students to meet and exceed expectations. Through Amyra Tutorial, she has been achieving her dream of doing more to reach low-performing students in order to achieve greater school and student success.

Culp graduated from Morris Brown College and Atlanta University with a master's degree and an Education Doctorate degree in Administration and Supervision. In addition, she graduated from the rigorous, two-year Georgia Superintendent Professional Development Program. She has conducted numerous workshops and training programs on classroom management, differentiated instruction and other topics of interest to educators.

She is married to the love of her life, Oscar, and they are the proud parents of two adult children, six grandchildren, and six great-grandchildren.

www.ingramcontent.com/pod-product-compliance
Lightning Source LLC
Chambersburg PA
CBHW030146240426
43672CB00005B/296